Praise for CEO of Yours

The bedrock of intelligent negotiating involves knowing... y precisely what you want, and how you may achieve those goals you deem most valuable. And Bart Jackson has created a practical, witty book that guides the reader in discovering the answers to all three of these vital elements. Never has the journey toward self-mastery been laid out more precisely and practically with a humorous wit that will keep you smiling all the way to success.

> – Greg Williams, *The Master Negotiator & Body Language Expert*

If only those mythical heroes of old had prepared their life's journey by reading Bart Jackson's CEO of Yourself, they might have easily overcome their existential challenges, have been guided to their treasure with the precision of a GPS, and enjoyed the journey with the entertaining wit and stories of a hero who has been there and back.

> – Senator Bill Golden

Thoroughly enjoyable and instructive, this book has helped me already in my quest to plan the remaining years of my career and future retired life. Filled with practical and engaging ideas, the author leads the reader through self-assessment to recognition of their innate capabilities and talents. Then he provides encouragement and challenges ("broccoli moments") to take one to task in the cause of self-betterment. With wonderful tidbits and sayings, he takes you inside your soul and brings you out encouraged and ready to be your best self. Thanks Bart, I needed this.

> – Mark Reisman, *Senior Consultant, Merrill Lynch*

It's a shame they no longer ban books in Boston.

> – Val Matthews, *Solutions Architect, IBM*

Training people to achieve their goals involves preparing them mentally, physically, and emotionally. Instead of mere "Yes you can" cheerleading, this book lays it all out and says, "Here's how." The author doesn't just tell you you're marvelous, he takes you step, by mindset, by action, and makes you prove it to yourself. In a straightforward, always fun style, each chapter arms you with the blueprint and powers you need on your individually chosen journey. And most refreshing, this is not a makeover book. It coaches and shows you that you already possess everything necessary to achieve the character you desire, and the goals you want to achieve. A vital empowerment guide. You need it. You'll enjoy it.

> – Ramona Braganza, *Celebrity Fitness Trainer, Founder, 3-2-1 Empower*

Growing up my father typically called me Boss. Not really understanding at five years old, later in life I would identify boss as someone who tells others what to do. After reading CEO of Yourself, I realized that the best boss isn't the one who tells others what to do but actively listens and uses that information to tell himself what to do. This book helped me in my adult years to understand I am my own man – and my own brand, and that I first must understand me. This is a page-turner and a vital guide for the young and old. I'm so glad I found it!

– Bruce Boyd, *Founding CEO, Building Our Youth Development*

Self-reliance and self-management are quintessentially American life skills – inherent in American individualism. Any one of us can be President or Chief Executive Officer. The CEO is virtually untrammeled in her decision-making power, but there is no one else to blame if those decisions do not produce. Bart Jackson brilliantly and instructively combines these two concepts of self-reliance and no-one-else-to-blame to help us identify and make good choices in our own lives and careers. As he says, "The choice, my friend, is truly yours".

Bart Jackson tells us how to be conscious and realistic about unlimited but not unconstrained choice. First, we must consider ourselves to be absolutely marvelous. (There's a whole chapter on that.) Then we must be capable of identifying the array of choices available. Then, there is attitude. Bart tells us how to establish and sustain attitudes over time – our character. This author is uniquely qualified to deliver these insights. He has interviewed and studied more on-the-job CEOs than anyone else in America. His data is vast and impeccably sourced. Secondly, he has mastered the art of turning his data into meaningful insights for you. How? By understanding what is going on in your head, in your life. It's an incredible skill, and you'll realize Bart Jackson's gift as you read this deeply-researched book.

– Hunter Hastings, *CEO, Economics for Business*

Bart Jackson scrapes the barnacles of habit away. He urges us to develop a win-win relationship with ourselves. It is a refreshing, energizing way to look at yourself and your most precious resource, your time. It is humbling and challenging. It reminds you that today is the first day of the rest of your life.

– Alfred R. Berkeley, *Director, World Economic Forum, USA*

Other Books by Bart Jackson include...

❖ The Art of the CEO

❖ Behind Every Successful Woman is Herself

❖ Business Basics

❖ So That's How They Do It
   – Tactics from Business Masters

❖ 101 Best Business Quips

❖ 102 Best Business Quips

❖ In the Words of My Wife's Husband
   – The complete sourcebook of business humor

❖ Whitewater
   – Running The Wild Rivers of North America

❖ The Garden State Wineries Guide

You may also enjoy...

❖ The Art of the CEO Radio Show

❖ BartsBooks Quips Newsletter

To purchase and learn more about the author's works
we invite you to visit our website **BartsBooks.com**

CEO of
Yourself

Getting Down to the Business of Your More Rewarding Life

By Bart Jackson

Published by

ULTIMATE BUSINESS GUIDES

A division of Prometheus Publishing, LLC

Published in the United States by
Prometheus Publishing, LLC
Please address all queries to Prometheus Publishing,
18 Petty Rd., Cranbury, New Jersey 08512

Prometheus Publishing books are now available at special rates for bulk purchases, and in digital and audio formats. Contact the publisher at the above address.

ISBN – 13: 978-0-692-98807-7

© January, 2021
BartsBooks Ultimate Business Guides
Prometheus Publishing, LLC

*To my father, Tom Jackson
who quietly, joyfully forged
his own unique life path,
then gently armed his son with
the tools to do the same.*

Foreword

Ayn Cates Sullivan, Ph.D.
President of Infinite Light Publishing & Media

I met Bart Jackson in New York City several years ago during Book Expo America. I soon realized with delight that we share a deep love of mythology. Bart Jackson is an expert in Greek & Roman Mythology, and you will notice that the ancient ones influence this book. I firmly believe in the importance of teaching ethics and life skills through storytelling. As Joseph Campbell taught in his book *Hero with a Thousand Faces*, people in all cultures relate to the hero or heroine's journey. For the wisdom of the ages to continue to pass forward into the next age, each generation needs to retell the myths in their own way. In this retelling of a myth, the relevance is born again.

CEO of Yourself is based in ancient wisdom that has been redesigned for the current era. Bart Jackson reminds us that life and livelihood are connected. We are the ones who know how to make our life more rewarding. We know what choices we need to make. Bart Jackson believes that we can learn to handle each life situation we encounter with more genius, hammering out our own unique guiding principles. He reminds us that character is important and that we can use our free will to create more exciting lives.

When Bart Jackson approached me about writing the foreword to *CEO of Yourself*, I decided to take some time with the book. I took his lead and did a tour of myself, examining my best qualities, as well as my desires. We all know our weaknesses, but Bart also suggests that we explore the ways in which we truly excel. I found the inquiry helpful and scribbled many notes on the pages of the book. For many years it has been clear to me that when we understand which archetypal energy we are working with, it becomes easier it is to understand the challenges that we must face and overcome on our hero's journey. Most of us have an archetype that is closely related to our mission. Thinking about this material, I can see that most of my work has indeed been touched by Athena and her genius of bringing light to civilization. In some mysterious archetypal way, I am working in service to the brilliant daughter of Zeus.

In this fast-paced and ever-changing world, we often are required to become the heroes and heroines of our lives, even showing up as our own Chief Executive Officer. Emerging entrepreneurs seek true templates for success, and I think Bart Jackson's CEO of Yourself is one of the prototypes we can trust. Bart Jackson actively encourages the reader to redefine their Mission Statement and step onto life's broad stage with a CEO's adventurous perspective.

As I read CEO of Yourself, I thought about the archetypes that Bart mentions in passing, as well as the universal truths behind them. Theseus, the adventurous hero, mythical king, and founder of Athens appears in these pages, acting as an invisible guide throughout the book. Theseus knows how to move deftly from one age to another and survive. As we tap into this archetype, we can utilize a similar thread of wisdom. With the help of the good princess Ariadne, Theseus was able to slay the dangerous Minotaur, the half man – half bull monster who lived in a labyrinth. In other words, since Theseus learned how to weave his own destiny, he was able to overcome almost insurmountable odds, succeed and become a hero and eventually a king. All heroes and heroines are challenged, and that's the point. The plight of Ariadne is also entangled in this book, because she understands the glittering threads of our unfold- ing destiny. In modern parlance, we would say she knows how to walk through the mazes of our time and succeed. In fact, Theseus would not have made it without her. As these pages remind us, we are stronger and wiser when we team up.

In CEO of Yourself, once we know who our guide is, who we are, and what our business calling or vision might be, then we explore the platform from which our ideas grow. This is an important part of Bart Jackson's teaching, because if we wish to have a thriving, successful, conscious business that serves humanity, then we need to be aware of our beliefs and principles. Each chapter in this book has an area to clarify your archetype, mission, and values.

Influential people serve to support or limit our evolution. We each have a signature tune, and the theme of CEOs emerges as clearly as a song when working through the pages of the book. With a solid foundation built on your ethics, a vision of your enriched life, with all its possibilities emerges. As Bart Jackson explains, all CEOs need to create a vision and then a course of action. Our job as CEOs of ourselves is to assemble resources, which includes myth, enlist aid, and then design our life. The map is clear, and the sketch through the maze is our own.

Prometheus must also be mentioned here, for he stole fire from the gods and gave it to humanity in the form of intelligence. Although he was frowned upon by the immortals, he is one of the great champions of humankind. Prometheus was punished, but Chiron freed him in the end. The story reminds me that humanity cannot survive alone, and that in order to succeed we need good foundations, wisdom, and helpful friends. Together we can birth a new humanity. Bart Jackson provides us with timeless roads to success that have survived the centuries, with a bit of humor tossed in for good measure. ▩

Table of Contents ∿

Acknowledgements

Kudos to those many generous individuals who with their advice and by their examples have contributed to these pages. Your insights have been the making of this book.

My greatest appreciation to editor Christian Kirkpatrick, whose immense personal wisdom and penetrating understanding of the English language have given stronger wings to the ideas I have struggled to present.

Sincerest thanks and praise to Dorothy Amsden, whose matchless, intuitive graphic artistry and artwork bring light to every page of text and joy to the reader.

Special blessings to Ms. Carol Ezzo, whose unflagging devotion nudged this author through endless surgeries and befuddlement to bring this book to you. Thanks for your belief.

Finally, heartfelt thanks to my good wife Lorraine, who not only edits her husband's works, she edits him. ▣

❧ **Introduction** ❧

Since no one ever reads introductions, I feel fairly free to unvarnish the truth right here, at the outset. The pages that follow strew broccoli over a path already paved with donuts. That is, they put forth an exceptionally effective, but not always attractive, solution to achieving your goals.

Browse the bookstore shelves today. They sag with volumes colorfully condensing life's answers into Seven Easy Theses, Nine Happy Habits, The Four-Step Sigma Success Process, and on and on. Unfortunately, authors have somehow fallen into the mythstep that their countless years of hard experience and probing research must be burnished into a quick-click message, brief as a pre-prandial wine toast and as effortlessly mantled as a new necktie. Meanwhile, sales-starved publishers boast, "Well, my life-solution book is even simpler than yours."

Of course, such dumbing down is an insult to you, the reader. Yet even more important than belittling your good mind, those who would sell you salvation with merely 15 minutes a day or 10 commandments are cheating. Life, business, or darned little else that's worthwhile may not be mastered with a recipe. Happily, your days on this terrestrial orb hold too many flabbergastingly unanticipated variables to "scientifically" confine them within algorithm or formula. Best to dump such plodding, preprogrammed formulae onto your app-laden phone – and hit "delete."

Much of my life as a journalist has been spent chatting with explorers, entrepreneurs, and business leaders to learn their personal art of accomplishment. They are not all happy. They do not all possess any common trait. And each seems to have come to her or his success via markedly separate routes.

For years this very lack of commonality kept puzzling me. Terry Bollard, among other astounding solo expeditions, circumnavigated Australia by kayak. The equally courageous Mel Duncan founded the Nonviolent Peaceforce, which trains and places completely unarmed protectors in war-torn areas to halt the rape, pillage, and slaughter of civilians. Each of these gentlemen chooses his attitudes, emotions, and planning methods from an entirely different palate. Even corporate CEOs Eric Schmidt (Google), Denise Morrison (Campbell Soup), and Al Berkeley (NASDAQ) guide their enterprises and themselves with techniques more reflective of their individual characters than of any standard business practice. And that individuality, I finally realized, is the whole point. (Like Buddha beneath his Bodhi tree and Isaac Newton beneath his apple tree, my far more humble bit of enlightenment fell upon me while laboring 'neath the vines of my grape arbor. But no matter.) Though their ventures may be similar and certain challenges may seem nearly identical, each achiever I interviewed saw the choices available to her/him. Each one set the stage so that he might bring the full advantage of his own distinct batch of abilities to bear. These folks arrived at their amazing accomplishments by magic – the deft blending of science (a specific set of repeatable formulae) with art (their personal gifted and cultivated abilities). And that is where the broccoli comes in.

Magic takes work. Work that, while it is very good for you, is not always tasty. Famed escape magician Harry Houdini devoted days to studying the science of locks and vaults. He innovated miniaturized tools for defeating them. He trained for countless hours, teaching his tough, athletic body to contort and even untie knots with his toes. Knowing that the deed alone was not enough, Harry, with the help of his wife Bess, became a wizard at marketing his magical escapes and drew enormous crowds. Houdini blended his personal, trained artistry with the optimum scientific methods of the day. So then, within minutes of being manacled, cinched into a straight jacket, and locked into the city jail – presto! The amazing Harry Houdini could bound onto the theatre stage and take his bows, acknowledging the wildly enthusiastic applause of a bewildered audience. It's all magic, but it is not either instantaneous or easy.

Jeff Bezos, after watching Internet usage expand at the rate of 2,300 percent annually, chose to take the entrepreneurial leap and launch an online bookstore. And presto! Amazon bounds onto the global stage as the e-commerce leader, making Jeff the world's richest man. (Or perhaps we should say, "Cadabra," since that was the company's original name.) Yet under any sobriquet, the 25-year achievement of

Amazon is no mere wave of the wand. It has come to pass through the magic of Mr. Bezos' personal inventive artistry carefully tempered and forged with the best managerial techniques of our times.

Like Harry and Jeff, each of us makes a little magic every day. In that special way only you can, you wrench a few recipes from memory, stir them in with those abilities and styles unique to you, and voila! You accomplish. You create dinner, a deal, an expedition, or an act of love. And the prize goes to that wizard who can consistently make magic that fulfills her own self. She conjures best who pleases herself best.

After all, your first duty is to yourself. And my greatest wish for your own true self is that you don't worry, do sweat, and joyously experience that highest of all possible human states – enthusiasm. BB

– Bart Jackson

Author's Note

In this our second edition, we are responding to readers' requests, with two hopefully helpful additions.

First, in order to make this a working guide, at the end of each section, we are providing a "My Thoughts" space for you to add your own notes and replies to some of our thought prompters. There is something magical about pushing a pen across an open page. The concepts we conjure seem to hold a finer point and stick with us more meaningfully. So as you forge your own pathway toward fulfillment, we invite you to employ these pages to jot down those mental sparks that will be of value to remember.

Secondly, at book's end, you will find One Final Adventure: The Entrepreneurial Employee. Urged by audiences at several of the author's speaking events, this wrap-up section focuses all the previous pages on the single challenge of the workplace. The perception of the salaried employee striding into the workplace with an entrepreneur's venture-launching mindset connects naturally the Self CEO building the Enterprise of You. Much of the support and tactics for this section have come from Dr. Dale Caldwell's Entrepreneur Zones Movement, on whose advisory board it is my great privilege to serve. Also, my many thanks to the exemplary achievers profiled in this section. They are the individuals who add excitement and inspiration to the entire business community.

– Bart

SECTION I

Creating the Vision

Chapter 1

You as Chief Executive Officer

Becoming a CEO is less like ascending a learning curve and more akin to stepping off a ledge and attempting to fly. – BJ

Let us be very honest with ourselves. You want to grab more out of life. You get only one trip 'round this terrestrial orb, and you know – you just know – there lies a richer experience than you are getting.

Well, who is planning your life thus far? Your spouse? Friends? Governors of your workplace or nation? Fate? God? Some entrenched creed? Or perhaps, yourself? If your answer is All of the Above, how much of a final governing hand belonged to you in those planning decisions? Most of us spend most of our lives operating in default mode. We don't make the choices that would deliver that richer life into our hands, simply because we don't know the choices exist – or we don't realize they are ours to make.

So what's on your wish list? What would you like to do or have in your life that currently just isn't happening? In preparation for writing this book, we surveyed hundreds of individuals, asking those two questions. Their replies came with startling rapidity. Most folks knew very well what would enrich their lives.

We share a small sampling of their answers:
Well, if I really could decide, I know exactly what I'd like....

▶ Some real appreciation and respect at work. Uncalculated praise coming my way in a career I feel is truly taking off.

▶ Without a doubt, more time peacefully creating in my garden. Maybe I would cultivate a small vineyard.

- Good friends – I mean real back-slapping buddies who meet all the time, share the important stuff, and have fun just being together.

- Testing and taking myself to new limits. Doing some tough, high-altitude climbing in Tibet. And biking from Lhasa to Kathmandu.

- Holding some honest influence with others. I'd like to feel that my words and work matter – and possess the power to move people.

- (Our favorite) Waking up happy. You know, waking up singing – billowing the shower curtain with bellowsome tones merry enough to blush my teenage daughter crimson with embarrassment.

- And of course, more time. Precious, precious time to study, start that business, read, chat, finally write that book, stroll, travel, sip coffee over the paper, and feel that the entire day was mine to feast upon.

Each of these separate goals is a good life step. But pursuing just one upgrade is like trying to create vintage wine by randomly squeezing grapes as you stroll amongst the vines. If you want your soul to savor fully for a lifetime, you will have to invest a large dollop planning, a little organized process, and a hefty shot of leadership. In short, you need to view your own marvelous self as an energetic enterprise of which you will take charge and will operate as CEO.

Chief Executive Officer

Why assume this title? It is an apt reflection of the power you possess over that body, intellect, and spirit that compose you. You are more than president – one who presides over all that happens around you. You are less powerful than dictator. Frankly, when poet William Ernest Henley asserted, "I am the master of my fate. I am the captain of my soul." he overreached. You may well be the captain of your soul, but you are not the master of your fate. We all lie in the clutch of circumstance. Stuff happens. As CEO of yourself or of a company, it becomes your duty to handle that environment swirling around you and actively enlist all available resources to make the best of it. 'Tis take-charge time.

Consider your title:

Chief – You gather all your assets and helpers on your team, directing them toward your created vision.

Executive – You initiate and oversee all action. Even events you don't perform with your own hands get launched because you give the sign to "make it so."

Officer – The good Lord has invested you with the authority and responsibility to make every possible decision regarding your actions.

Taking on the mantle of Chief Executive Officer of Yourself is no mere catchphrase. As CEO:

▶ You assess and evaluate your situation and resources.

▶ You create a vision and a product – then set goals to fulfill both.

▶ You decide on courses of action and reaction you deem practical and achievable.

▶ You enlist advisors and acting agents.

▶ You assemble the resources and all necessary fundraising for additional resources to accomplish given goals.

▶ You move forward. Achieving initial goals, you publicize them and employ them as fuel for future goals and further visions.

All of this blend of insight and oversight brings a new power. How much power? Don't get too heady here. Real power is as fleeting as romance in a brothel. Flashes of it come your way only unexpectedly. Yet as you undertake a CEO's perspective and duties, you will lay bare a strength that's lain dormant too long. "Yeah, yeah, yeah, I can handle that," says your spirit. You'll cut the strings and laugh at the fool who pretends to be your puppeteer. You will observe creeping into your worldview, as Mark Twain so eloquently put it, the calm confidence of a Christian with four aces. And that self-mastery will bring a justified smile to your lips.

In addition to unleashing this personal power surge, viewing your life role as chief executive officer opens access to the best method we *Homo sapiens* have developed thus far for accomplishing things. Over the ages of taking our lumps and struggling for survival, humankind has groped around and experimented with countless ways for bringing about what we want in this life. And we keep coming back to that process that keeps delivering success.

You as Chief Executive Officer

The Business Method

Business is the way we humans get things done. It also is the primary way we decide what to do and what's important. It is business that spans the globe with connective highways and transforms the Internet from geek theory into a contributing tool that assists our lives, and continues to improve.

Business presses knowledge into action to fulfill human needs. Further, it aggressively develops ways to connect the deed or product with everyone who might benefit from it. Medical research gets turned into life-saving drugs. Experiment emerges as service. By the 1880's, scientists such as Oliver Lodge had proved that radio waves could be transmitted and received across distant open space. The papers were written and impressive demonstrations made. But it took Mr. Guglielmo Marconi and his cousin to form The Wireless Telegraph & Signal Company and make wireless communication transmission a publically used, effective service to humanity.

This semi-systematized process by which we form and run businesses is neither rigid nor precise. Unlike the scientific method, you will not find it charted step-by-step in textbooks. But it does possess an ancient pedigree with a currently unbeaten track record. To best comprehend how the business method works, let us step back and take a fanciful look at one of humankind's first entrepreneurial ventures.

Like all businesses, this one begins with desire. Some Paleolithic flint chipper wants to eat better, and so does everyone else in his clan. In his travels, he stumbles across a chunk of hard, sharp-edged obsidian. Sometimes the human need searches out a solution; sometimes the solution sparks awareness of the human need. Either way, a visionary entrepreneur and a structured enterprise are born.

▶ Our entrepreneur squints at the stone and imagines sharper new blades that will bring down more tasty game and will slice it up more rapidly.

▶ Through trial and error he pounds out a sharp obsidian stone point. He brings forth his creation expecting to swap his way into riches. No one wants it. He has failed. His time is wasted.

- Our entrepreneur decides to enlist aid. He sets the clan's two best point-sculptors to work. (The seeds of labor negotiation consultants, HR recruiting firms, and managerial motivational books get sown.) The entrepreneur sends his swift-footed daughters to search out and bring back more, better quality obsidian. (Supply chain enterprises, caravans, and customs collectors all await in the wings.)

- Value is assessed and development occurs. Better points urge the manufacture of better arrow and spear shafts. Companies form to send sailors on earth-spanning, dangerous voyages to procure nutmeg and spices to preserve the increased food supply delivered by the new weaponry. Captains, surgeons, and naval architects study these ventures and find ways to reduce their danger. Meanwhile, back home company owners are busy convincing commoners and kings that spice satchels will actually save meat, cure plague, and win ROI. (Marketing spins slightly beyond control.) Each businessperson plays her part, poorly at first, then, with input of others, better and better. And so things get accomplished. Useful products are produced, reshaped, and distributed for the benefit of all. In the end, many heirs of our Paleolithic flint-chipping entrepreneur do swap their way into riches. Enter financial advisors.

This prehistoric fable of the business method only lightly skims its surface. Yet notice a few strengths. The business method operates in real life. Failure is foreseen and accommodated as merely a mandate for change. The quest is limitless, because the vision is expanding. Better materials are sought as widely as possible, until some new product fills the desire. Every structure is erected with the assumption of future improvement. Assessments are continually made to determine how far and how well we've gone today, plus what more and better efforts will serve tomorrow. Advancement is the byword. Such are the strengths that will benefit your own method of developing yourself, and such is the method that can best guide you on your journey.

So when you ask, "What am I going to do with ME – this magnificent human biomachine that has recently reached the age of decision?" Why not conduct your life along this high-achievement model of business that has proven itself over the ages? And why not rephrase that question as, "How am I going to run this enterprise of ME?"

Catching the Beat

This was exactly the question young Lisa Pegher put to herself. At age 11 in a blue-collar, Pennsylvania town, Lisa selected the drums as her creative vehicle. Without any of the high-end equipment or, initially, any of the top-flight mentoring, Lisa recalls that she "had to use whatever came to hand. I had to become inventive and go my own way." Lisa set her musical goals – her product aims. She developed a practice schedule and technique designed to invent her own original and alluring sound.

Most blossoming artists end up putting themselves in the hands of someone else. Musicians are notorious for turning "all the details" over to some agent (e.g., where I will play, with whom, what music and presentation methods will make me most appealing, what I will wear, and when will I be where?) This freedom from deciding ironically leads to a loss of nearly all other freedoms. Countless musicians burrow in, practice their craft, and become exactly what they have chosen to be: a property. But not Ms. Pegher.

Designing her training as a solo percussionist, Lisa forced percussion out from the back row, onto the virtuoso position at front stage center of the nation's top symphonies. The hidebound symphonic establishment, witnessing her peerless talent and audience appeal, avidly began seeking out this flamboyantly colorful, cutting-edge performer.

Today, Lisa Pegher has been named one of the top six performers of her generation. She has worked with agents yet currently finds them too sluggish in fulfilling her grand musical plan. When existing works were inadequate to showcase her talent and themes, Lisa enlisted composers like the internationally prominent Richard Danielpour to write works in coordination with her. (Listen to The Wounded Healer concerto.)

To fulfill her vision and expand her client base, Lisa has created a new band, aptly named Controlled Chaos. Lisa may appear Friday evening in concert with the Boston Symphony and on Saturday with her band in a coffee house before appreciative avant-garde listeners.

Like many entrepreneurs, Lisa Pegher developed her business and herself simultaneously. As CEO of each, she continues to grow both. Without any fixed checklist, Lisa employs the holistic process we call the business method.

Tips & Tasks The point of Lisa Pegher's tale is not her enviable success, nor her formidable talent. Rather, consider the number of choices this individual seized along her path to fulfillment. Much like yours, Lisa's failures were and are too numerous to list. Nor did circumstance groom her for this current outcome. As CEO of herself, she stood realistically before her situation. She assessed it, envisioned advancements, selected actions, enlisted aid. And today, as much as possible, Lisa governs her own course.

Broccoli Moments As anyone who has ever launched a business can attest, managing your own enterprise is one of the most rewarding ways you can expend your labor, sweat, and anxiety. (Whether it involves less work than slipping into default mode and letting others boss your actions is debatable.) Nonetheless, being chief executive officer of yourself demands hea$ doses of hard thinking and unexciting tasks with uncertain outcomes. You may call such toils the price of freedom or an investment in success. We have labeled them broccoli moments – things that are very nourishing and very good for you, even if they are not terribly yummy.

To you belligerent vegans out there, we mean no disrespect to your taste buds. We merely are bowing to the vast majority. Take note: donut and pastry chain stores flourish by the thousands. But not one successful broccoli chain comes to mind that thrives in our nation today – yet.

Just remember, that every game-winning touchdown pass tossed before cheering thousands by an NFL quarterback has been preceded by the countless hours of pushups and other tedious calisthenics that made it possible. 'Tis broccoli moments that prepare for glory.

As CEO of yourself you will make the choices, design your days, and handle the flow of fate in ways that will allow you to grab more out of life. Will they win you that respect, those good friends, that vineyard, or a joyous morning song that mortifies your daughter? If that's what you truly seek, may it be so. You will certainly be bettering your odds. And there is a virtual guarantee that you will think a whole lot better of yourself.

So now that you've accepted the title and privileges of chief executive officer, let's create that individual you need to be. **BB**

You as Chief Executive Officer

Afterthought ∿

At age 15 he began listing them: write a book, paddle the Nile River, meet the president, learn touch typing, live with pygmies, climb the highest mountains... 127 accomplishments. Wrapped in the enthusiasms of youth, John Goddard beheld all the earth as an exciting challenge. Like all lads, he dreamed dreams, but in John's case he took the two next giant steps that would lead him into one of the most adventurous and fulfilling lives any person could hope to enjoy. First stride: he developed a vision. John sorted through his boyhood fantasies and transformed certain ones into defined, achievable goals. Secondly, he laid out courses of action that led him to attain them.

For John Goddard, this written list became his own life. Like most CEOs, John's were days of envisioning, planning, plunging, conquering, failing, and striving again. He adopted a lilies-of-the-field approach to living. John faced kayaking the 4,145 miles of the Nile River, source to mouth, with no previous paddling experience. He grabbed nearly all the necessary training as needed, on the fly. Adequate finances came from his lectures and two books, Kayaks Down the Nile and The Survivor. It is surprising how often the planned and passionate pursuit of what a person truly desires steamrolls over obstacles and brings fulfillment beyond the achievement.

Chapter 2

Your Marvelous Self

*The creations and feats
of humankind forever amaze me.
Yet I find even more astounding
each individual's sheer audacity
at attempting them.* – BJ

If you do not find yourself to be absolutely marvelous, you just are not looking hard enough. Or you are not looking in the right rooms of your house. Or perhaps your vision is darkened by the shadow of others.

Every one of us slips wriggling and screaming into this life already clutching a great wealth of talents, each waiting to be discovered and developed. From the very first moment we grip Daddy's finger in the birthing room, others begin to boast of our powerful potential. A bit biased and overeager perhaps, the family will devote the next months to hovering, watching for any slight indication of telltale acts that indicate the infant's future glories. (As a newborn who tipped the hospital scales at 10 pounds, eight ounces, this author's career in the NFL as a fullback vs. point guard was hotly debated.)

With this same innocence and energy, reflect on your many talents. Take a tour of yourself. Recall those episodes when you easily turned your hand to something – took apart and reassembled Uncle Sid's computer or made an impromptu speech that everyone applauded. Run through that long list of your achievements and see if you can pull out a thread of skills frequently employed. No paper, no lists. Set aside any thoughts of how your talents fit into any specific career or product package. Your abilities, after all, stand too vast and varied to be hemmed into a single action course. For now, you are basically trying to inventory your many:

▶ **Strengths** – things at which you excel (e.g., analytic problem solving, running, speaking, negotiating, rapid mental and physical reactions).

- **Proclivities** – behaviors and actions you tend toward (e.g., humor, achieving consensus, finding universal themes, physical activity).

- **Interests** – activities you enjoy delving into and that make you forget the time (e.g., woodworking, computer logic, listening to and encouraging others).

This is just a stroll through memory to see what assets you have lying around the warehouse today. Of course, all these strengths, interests, and even the proclivities evolve.

Proclivities are vital because they reveal abilities that you might not realize as valuable personal assets. Are you an aural learner tending to take the latest computer instruction from the mouth of an expert rather than from his manual? You've probably honed the ability of distilling the essence of a speaker's ramblings. Are you the kind of person folks come to with their troubles? You may hold unrealized powers of human perception and persuasion. Remember, you naturally lean toward what you enjoy and what brings you success.

What Good Is That?

Elaine is a careful, cogent attorney in one of the largest, most influential commercial law firms in Illinois. She knows how to flex the spoken and written word in ways that invariably benefit her clients. Scrupulously honest and quietly businesslike, Elaine lets her deeds speak for her, and they have spoken well enough to make her one of the most sought-after partners in her firm. Her assisting attorney, James, is an effusive social butterfly who invariably tends to schmooze with everyone within earshot. Elaine had always found James' antics, as she called them, oddly amusing. Then one day, on a convention floor, she took the time to witness her assistant in action. James, as usual, was yukking it up, the center of conversation, holding the rapt attention of four other laughing folks, two of whom Elaine recognized as leaders of major manufacturing firms. Each one in this tight clutch leaned in closely, eagerly answering the questions James put to them. Cards were passed back and forth.

A few days later, Elaine received a call from one of the manufacturers, asking her advice. As it turned out, James' loyalty matched his verbosity. He always carried a bundle of Elaine's business cards in his pocket. And amid his swapping of stories about wines, travel destinations, and sports team screwups, James invariably injected off-the-cuff tales of Elaine's legal triumphs.

"I had never viewed James' mannerism as an ability," Elaine confessed to me later. "I always thought he was just a talker who liked to chatter. I never realized that such socializing actually might be a developed and useable skill." Elaine's response is understandable. It is difficult to view a style so foreign to your own as anything but a mere individual characteristic. Conversely, it's probable that James found Elaine's agonizing over each word in a deposition as only "the boss's fussiness."

Have you seen any admirable skills expressed in the proclivities of those around you? Would it be worth stepping out of your comfort zone to adopt them?

Blunders to Avoid Beware the labeling trap. You perform several very successful sales-boosting deeds that the marketing managers praise as extremely valuable. So you begin thinking of yourself as a great marketer. Fine, as far as it goes. But is that label all you are good for? Don't your skills hold a broader reach?

When you begin slicing up and cramming your abilities into boxes, you tend to cut off the shark's fin and throw the rest of the animal away. Your initial duty as CEO of Your Marvelous Self is to realize all your attributes and unleash all their potential. There is no junk DNA.

From Assets to Enterprise

As you begin to inventory your many assets, the truth will doubtless occur to you. You are not a kitchen-table startup. You are an intricate, vastly connected corporation in the truest sense. Your many interacting parts, unceasing fountain of ideas, and exquisitely motivating emotions bring more exploits into your imagination than you could ever launch into action. Your one life is too short for all your dreams and abilities. You are both source and resource. You hold more concepts and have at the ready more experientially grounded wisdom than any mere computerized program. And we haven't even gotten to your supporting cast of allies yet.

Guiding this sprawling avalanche of potential and desires toward a richer life experience is going to take some shoving, molding, and planning. Your multi-faceted Marvelous Self requires some unified trajectory and leadership. Without it, you will drift forever on a sea of whimsy. Crafting a solid vision will get things kickstarted.

And please, keep it lofty. You seek more than a single, glorious venture. We are shooting for an enriched life that fulfills the soul with inspiring memories, eager undertakings, and tantalizing goals. Such a life path demands a sustained perspective. It is high time to make the shift from what you want to do, to who you want to be. 'Tis time to envision yourself as a questing, complete enterprise, led from venture to adventure by a daring chief executing officer who corrals all of you, interjecting energy and direction.

Sound fanciful? In plain terms, it boils down to readying your mind for digging in and getting what you really want out of life. And the organizational pattern? Employ that proven business method mentioned earlier. Go with what works. And who'll provide the leadership? You seem the obvious choice, but to confirm, let's step inside yourself again and take a look at your resume.

CEO of Yourself

Your Secret Resume

The tour of yourself you made at the start of this chapter demonstrated a boatload of capabilities. Yet you far exceed the total of all the things you are good at. Our inventory shows you also possess an impressive list of intangible leadership qualities:

▶ **Intellectual Curiosity** Don't you just love that book or video clip that reveals some fascinating factoid or insight? Despite our culture's insistence that you buckle down and focus, your desire to explore still sparks your mind to a wider view.

▶ **Ability to Plan** You routinely juggle work necessities, annoyances, transportation, family needs, fiscal planning, and vacation expeditions without breathing heavily. You have erected the framework and are ready for more.

▶ **Enthusiasm** You fall passionately in love with the right projects. Be it designing the perfect app or dinner party, riding forward on the whirlwind of your latest invention or spiritual revelation. When the cause strikes the right chord, you pull out all the stops and accomplish whatever needs to be done.

▶ **Dependability** You also possess that vital willingness to grind along, follow orders, and work alongside disagreeable individuals all for the sake of getting the job done.

▶ **Readiness to Learn** You look for a better way – compare new methods against old. When you discover some personal strength, you strive to improve and share it everywhere it can be of use.

▶ **Creative Energy** You are bubbling over with it. It comes innately with our *Homo sapiens* tool kit. Progress and achievement are among your greatest thrills. They form a beneficial addiction of which you seldom seem to dine your fill.

Yes, you have all these attributes. Now, for the fun of it, reread your secret resume as a human resources executive reviewing candidates. What do you sound like? OMG! This is the person I want to hire. What a great employee. What a great CEO in training.

The point of this fantasy resume is that, know it or not, you possess the seed. You have what it takes to forge the life you want. And what will that be? That's your choice.

Client Satisfaction

You have toured the warehouse and found more than ample resources. There's some fabulous stuff in there. You've reviewed the resumes and discovered ideal leadership with all the expertise and experience to create a fine product – actually, a stellar product. Normally, the next step should be to show this prototype concept around in hopes of dredging up potential clients. But there is a bit of a blip in this case. You are the client. The new and improved self you are ramping up to produce must be, above all, pleasing to you alone. Additionally, you are also the CEO. That should make it easy, shouldn't it? No surveying, no testing. The CEO instinctively knows what the client wants, doesn't he? Just follow gut instinct, right? Well, in truth, no. Not if you are wise.

All clients (you included) are whimsical. They want what they want today. If you listen to the voice of your inner client she will have you running around the vineyard squeezing this bunch of grapes, then that one, and that ideal vintage wine you have always desired will ever elude you.

Google did not grow huge by answering today's craving. Rather, its leaders studied and unearthed benefits of which future buyers had never dreamed, but definitely would enjoy tomorrow. Before creating a next generation Google Education System, the company's G-Suite team exhaustively studied infants and children to see the variety of ways they prefer to learn. Then they gathered and analyzed this information and Boom! Google comes out with a product that far exceeds expectations, and customers gleefully line up to purchase.

As chief executive officer, your goal is to develop a self that exceeds current desires and expectations. To reach this un-envisioned fulfillment you are going to have to construct your own principles and use them to develop your new character. It will take this powerful character to burst apart that default-mode cocoon and transform your marvelous self into an enthusiastic butterfly.

Tips & Tasks Please do not dismiss today's yearnings. Whether an age-old dream or a new passion, your immediate wants are not forever to be shelved in preference of some longer-term fulfillment. Today is the day to dust off your dream of basking in the artistic superlatives of Florence Italy, or climbing your state's highest mountain. Such exhilarating experiences may be gobbled up and used to fuel those longer range designs for your richer life.

Consider the Source

With all this peering inside and uncovering new powers, at some point, your curious mind will no doubt draw you into pondering the source of it all. Is my personal spirit fed by some greater fountain of spirituality? Are there connections possible?

These are thoughts that in their very asking are enriching. Whatever your conclusions, whether they lead toward any concept of cosmic divinity or not, the mere scrutiny brings pleasure and growth. May you yield to such investigations frequently and search out the findings of others. And as you proceed along this elevated quest, please take this author's wish that your spiritual resolutions not confine your dreams, but open them to further joy. **BB**

Afterthought

Law is such a Procrustean profession. Every specialized niche, protocol, and practitioner gets slotted into hidebound traditions with no more flexibility than a nun's vow. Sharp, aggressive, and extremely agile-minded, young attorney Sharon Mahn was scooped up by one of Manhattan's most prestigious law firms, launching her into a promising career. In short order, her legal acuity was evident, but her real star shown beyond her precedents. Sharon Mahn was a natural client magnet. Using her proclivity toward matchmaking, she would sing the praises of her fellow law firm members and entice scores of new clients into their offices. In Sharon's rookie year, she brought in more business than any of the veteran partners.

So, did the firm give Sharon a bonus for all this income? Of course not. "Sharon, my dear, we have protocols here," she was told. "You personally must perform the work for each client you enlist. You can't just traipse around inviting all kinds of paying customers to our door. Imagine the havoc that would wreak."

Fortunately, Sharon Mahn could not see the havoc for the profit. Thus, combining her strength of problem-solving compassion, her interest in connecting folks, and her learned legal skills, Sharon founded Mahn Consulting, LLC that recruits the foremost legal and C-suite talent for Fortune 100 firms. For the past decade Ms. Mahn has been rated as one of the top recruiters worldwide. On the side, Sharon continues to link donors with charities, entrepreneurs with funders, and those in need with those who've got. She glides smilingly through New York's most celebrated society with sincere kindness. Like most of us, Sharon Mahn possesses marvelous assets. Unlike most of us, she has carved out the optimum way to employ them all, bringing fulfillment to herself and others.

CEO of Yourself

My Thoughts...

A few thought starters, and
a little space to jot down
what's of value to remember.

Two things that would really enrich my life are...

As CEO of myself I would operate more effectively if I
could adopt these two (or more) attitudes...

Some of those strengths, interests, and proclivities that often lie hidden from others, and even myself, might include...

Oh my heavens. The real, honest reasons that get me out
of bed and off to work each morning are...

SECTION II

Creating Your Product

CEO of Yourself

Chapter 3

The Choices are Truly Yours

*Freedom is not a gift,
but a hunting license. Those who
would win it must open their eyes
wider and flex their hands
in readiness to seize it.* – BJ

Simple question: How much of what you did yesterday was deliberately selected from a wide array of options, and how much was performed unthinkingly, as merely a part of a repetitive routine?

Lee Jun-fan, whom most of us know as film actor Bruce Lee, learned the traditional form of Wing Chun self-defense as a youth. But he did not become the planet's premier martial artist by sticking strictly to the pathways of that ancient art. Instead, Bruce studied and incorporated 26 different styles of fighting in practice around the world. Training diligently in American boxing, French savate (foot-fighting), and others, he analyzed, selected, and adopted those elements that proved most useful. He then bound them into a single fighting system specifically tailored to his abilities and needs.

As a boy, Bruce Lee faced the initial choice: Wing Chun – do it or don't. Circumstance had given him the opportunity to devote himself to this new, exciting art. He chose to just do it. Then, early on, the young martial artist took the next step: he raised his goals and thus broadened his choices.

Bruce Lee took what current business jargon terms as "executive overview." He set aside the vision of himself as dedicated follower along a single, well-worn track. Instead, he sought a wider martial artistry that would give him mastery over his mind, body, and all opponents. Lee understood that to choose the best tools, he would have to aggressively explore and discover what was available.

When achieving your goal, examine the whole world of options before you. Masters are those individuals wise and brave enough to climb the mountain and:

▶ Realize the innumerable choices available.

▶ Select those components offering the best benefit.

▶ Execute them as practical solutions for each unique situation.

Bruce Lee was already a master of Wing Chun and karate at age 19 when he first brought his skills into the boxing ring. In a demonstration match, Golden Gloves boxer Leo Fong invited Lee to attack him. With a swift succession of rapid-fire, slicing chops Lee came charging at his opponent. Fong countered with a boxer's series of quick feints. He sidestepped the oncoming Lee, then pivoted to land a clobbering left hook. Both Bruce's body and ego took a definite beating that day. But the martial artist exited the ring with several new options. That encounter's lesson led Lee to meticulously pore over untold hours of boxing films. From this study, he emerged with an entire new attack stance, incorporating several original body-shifting techniques.

Most of us feel very little desire to climb the mountain to better view the wide field of life options below. It's not that we're lazy – far from it. By our very human nature we are a species of eager creators. Yes, you are. At the same time, we like to savor success. Accomplishment is a grand moment. It makes us hungry for more. So after you revel in your latest fulfillment for a bit, does it make sense to rise up from your laurels, do more of that exact same thing, and achieve more of that sweet taste of success? Follow the same old recipe? Well, up to a point.

Your life is your product. From the ceaseless river of circumstance flows a long, continuous stream of choices for you to make. To choose wisely you have to fully discern:

▶ The broad array of options flowing your way with each new event.

▶ That these options are yours for the choosing.

Default Man

Sadly, too many folks never even view their life as containing choices. The river of circumstance carries only boatloads of duties, shoulds, tasks to be done. From our youngest days we are told, "You can be anything you want to be – and here, my child, is what you want to be." Mom signs us up for karate classes because we want to grow strong and become disciplined. Dad urges us to join the traveling math team because it will help us be more acceptable to the right college.

Through these loving intentions filters down some vaguely understood goal that Mom and Dad really want for us. So, we all assume, it must be good. I had better buckle down and do it well. So I attend classes in which, much like home life, I follow the series of directives. It's not too bad. After all, rolling around with others on the mat is fun, and I look pretty cool in my new white karategi. They never let me box, though. They say it's barbaric, whatever that means.

In this society that dotes on and devotes so much to its children, the slim reed of free choice becomes swallowed up in a sea of guidance. With every hour of the youngster's time already spoken for, there seems little time or need for personal decision making. Add to this the constant bombardment of subtle and unsubtle persuasions discussed in the next chapter, and the child enters adulthood obediently living in default mode.

Default mode is easy. Seductively easy. One by one, when we're not even thinking about it, we outsource life's decisions to this individual and that institution. In return, we receive direction. We are freed from the bother of planning, uncertainty, and resistance. Days slide comfortably by.

We salve ourselves with assurances that "I am a devout Buddhist, good American, caring family man, loving wife, loyal employee," or whatever role. But such assurance provides only a brief Band-Aid. Beneath, the wound festers. We awake haunted by the suspicion that unseen others are forever pushing us around. We're angry, but not quite sure why. Our minds murmur back to us, "It's all gone terribly wrong somehow. I'm not doing what I want to do."

It is not that Default Man makes no choices. As fate sets a new situation or opportunity on his path, he chooses to either ignore it or turn the choice over to some wiser or convenient authority. The whole concept that I am the expert of what's best for me gets perverted into I know only what I want...others should decide what's best. You hear it all the time. Our daily conversations are riddled with resignation to this perceived powerlessness. Literally within a single month this author has heard folks utter these phrases:

▶ *I have to get up at 6:30 to be there at 8:45, when the boss wants everyone to arrive.*
Your boss does not dictate or give a hoot at what hour you greet the glorious morn. You can opt to rise at 5:45 – have a real breakfast, read a book, actually talk with your children. Who wrote that your day's launch must center around work?

▶ *I really hate to leave you guys just when things are getting interesting, but I'm sure my wife (pet, child, priest, mommy) must be stalking the floor by now. So I'll leave you to the fun.*
Your grinding guilt about snatching some personal enjoyment goes way beyond your spousal or pet relations. Best fix your head – then party on.

▶ *Literature really fascinates me. I'd love to study it, but I'm scared not to major in business. You know. It's really competitive to get a good job. (Spoken by a college freshman.)*
This new collegian who plans to subvert her love of learning for future earnings saddens my heart. Who stunted her life path with fear and choked it with job-first propaganda?

▶ *No, I can't make it Tuesday afternoon. Jimmy has a soccer practice, and they always want the parents to be there.*
My dear Soccer Mom, have you actually asked Jimmy if he wants you peering supportively over his shoulder? And oops! Are you just giving into peer pressure because "they" are doing it, Mom?

▶ *I really wanted that job in Idaho....nice promotion....would have been the making of my career, but you know, as the Good Book says, kids come first.*
Now here's an artificial choice: kids vs. career. Dad has determined that children can grow properly in only one narrow environment, that the father's fulfillment has no effect on his children, and worst of all, some "Good Book" authority has deemed sacrifice as necessarily noble. Poor Dad, so sad, you've turned down a family adventure and swallowed a confining creed with all the courses of unhappiness served with it.

CEO of Yourself

▶ **This woman in the gym was ranting against immigrants. Jenni and I were so angry we had to bite our tongues.**

Jenni was dying to shout, "Did you know, my misinformed bigot, that 48.7 percent of this decade's new businesses were launched by immigrants, and you want to send them where?" But no, she cannot say that; she was taught to be polite, never make a scene. Tell that to the itinerant Galilean preacher who angrily overturned the money changers' tables. The self-mutilization response to anger is always wrong. Select again.

▶ **I wrestle constantly with my faith. There are several parts that I just find difficult to accept.**

Has our faith wrestler ever wondered why he should wrench his will to believe any tenets of any creed, instead of formulating his own?

Sound familiar? You probably hear such mutterings all the time. In each case, the speaker betrays an apparent helplessness, followed by the merest hint of regret or resentment. And in each case the speaker's perceived "unavoidable" action has resulted from opting to deny or outsource her/his choices. Let's pull back the curtain on such anxiety-ridden comments and see what helplessness lurks in our own psyches.

Decisions, Decisions

All the previous situations offer the opportunity to choose. The CEO of Herself steps into the decision arena with two solid advantages. First, she carries one belief: whatever her vehicle, she alone holds the reins. Secondly, as CEO, she possesses the gift of goals. She guides an entity that is truly headed somewhere – somewhere she has selected. When daily choices are coupled with goals, the options proliferate. Witness this CEO's actual decision process.

The board chair, Doug, and CFO, Eileen, come into the CEO Sash's office and Doug asks:

So, what do you think, Sash?

Do we go with Eileen's plan to take our stock public and gear up for an IPO? Yes or no?

Sash looks Doug straight in the eye, and the wheels churn. He thinks:

My goal is to grow this company, which I already know requires more funding. So the question becomes what actions should I take that will

The Choices are Truly Yours

bring us the greatest funds most efficiently? Angels, venture capital, private equity? No, no, no. Too little and too many ties. Banks? No, they'll set us up for takeover with me on the curb. Yes, taking the stock to trade onto the public exchange is the most traditional and proven route, but let's look at the avenues....

Like Bruce Lee, Sash has done his research. He is ready to adopt the best elements. It is a question of how. So after seven seconds of private ponderings, he responds:

Definitely, the public market is our best answer. Eileen, I like what I've been studying on reverse mergers. Could you make me a candidates' list of currently publicly traded firms that we could team up with to get our stock on the public floor? Don't forget to feel out that GAB International that has been nosing around us. Doug, everyone knows that few guys have the IPO mechansims locked tighter than you. Could you check out some of your best investment houses – find the one that can get us through the procedure swiftly and, well, the way we want – you understand. So why don't we meet here Tuesday noon? We'll lunch in and hammer out a plan to take to the rest of the board.
Good call, Eileen.

What has just happened here? Sash has seamlessly transformed a choice into a new course of precise action. All the resources and the firm's best assets are brought into play, and the team is set off and running. Further, Sash did not bite on the cleft-stick choice presented him by Doug. For the CEO, decisions are almost invariably a spread of options, not light-switch binary: this or that, do it or don't. Even the world-weary Hamlet pondering whether "to be or not to be" realized there were more avenues open than the two he announces on the parapet. How do you want to be – and what?

Oceans of ink have been spilled enlightening folks on exactly how to make decisions. Actually, odds are excellent you already have a pretty good process churning within your own intellect. And the odds are even better that any author's personal template would not mesh with your mental machinery anyway. The only suggestion offered here is, after all is said and chosen, that you act kindly and cut yourself some slack. Whatever your decision earns, it is not your fault/credit alone. Remember what we noted earlier: you are not the complete master of your life. You are only the CEO.

CEO of Yourself

And Then There's FATE

Fate sits smilingly in your board chair seat. Much, though not all, of your CEO actions are made in response to the bludgeonings of circumstance that fate heaps upon you. Suppliers raise rates. Markets crash. Beethoven goes deaf. Samuel Clemens (Mark Twain) pours all his hard-earned fortunes into a revolutionary printing press that becomes outmoded by a more effective model hitting the market three months after his. Meanwhile, almost as a lark, Joe Ciacola posts an idea for his new "Watch Yo Mouth" game on social media and boom! Within 24 hours a stunned Joe has over 1000 orders even before he can put together a product.

The best-laid plans contort. Jeanne and Jan Murphy cleverly make a killing distributing a brand of golf gloves used by the top-winning pro on the circuit...until in the middle of the US Open. Then, for all the TV cameras to record, their endorsing pro misses a short putt, tears off his gloves, curses, hurls them to the ground and stomps on them. The Murphy's promotion and sales techniques had been flawless. But fate held other circumstances in store, and their profits screeched to a halt from that very moment.

Ask Sam, Ludwig, or the Murphys. There lies nothing noble in adversity. You don't require it to make you better. Having your dreams shattered and your laborious efforts turn to ashes is not good for you. It does not strengthen you. It does not improve your character any more than winning the lottery or inheriting Aunt Clara's billions. Your personal tempering and improvement springs from those reactions you choose to make. Your character is yours for the selecting.

So let there be no moaning at the bar – no whining, no soulful resignation, not even a slide into sadness. For such are the whisperings of defeat. And what comes out of your mouth you will slowly come to believe. Rather, let your lips curl back in a smile and brush off the heapings of fate like lint off flannel. Show yourself and your friends what you are made of. That is where nobility lies. The choice, my friend, is truly yours. ■■

Afterthought ∽

In the dark of night, actor Laurence Olivier stood calmly reflecting the glow of his newly built house as it burned to the ground before his eyes. He and his wife had barely escaped an accidental fire that was consuming everything they owned. As a single burning ash floated down at his feet, with Shakespearian aplomb the consummate thespian pulled out a cigarette, bent down, and used the ash to light it. Then, with a wry smile Olivier announced, "Well, at least I'm still getting some use out of this house." Now and again, dear reader, it helps to spit fate in the eye and set your mind onto your next chosen course.

CEO of Yourself

Chapter 4

Beggars at Your Door

*You are the prize
and trillions are spent
on winning you.* – BJ

By the thousands they come: institutions, religions, causes, workplaces, individuals, governments, advertisings, candidates. Each one reaches out, grasping for some piece of your precious self. They unleash an avalanche of solicitation urging the surrender of your body, cash, time, belief, vote, and even your devotion. As CEO, you see them for what they are: The Competition. You seek to govern yourself along the lines of your own, carefully determined goals. But the competition has other plans for your resources.

The numbers of these soliciting beggars are legion. Each day, the average person reveling in the delights of today's civilized realm, will encounter 3,000 persuasive messages entreating him to act in some way. (In 1970, it was 700.) Most solicitors are exquisitely capable in their seductions, and they have had a long head start. Since you first popped out of the womb, the competition has taken a firm grip on your ankle and is inching its way up your soul.

Sound melodramatic? We are sorted into rule-rich tribes from birth. Before she is old enough to cogently respond, the child is taught that she is a Jew and an American. Adults rhetorically ask, "You want to be a good Jew, don't you? A good patriotic American?" By the time we are able to intelligently self-direct, we realize that this established competition has already gained a great market share, and we are scrapping along as the entrepreneurial underdog. But don't get too upset. Every enterprise launches and labors under these same conditions. Now is your time to flick these competitors aside.

It's not easy to recognize them as beggars, even though that's what they are. Governmental propagandists do not whine miserably for your patriotic allegiance like some Cairo street beggar pleading for baksheesh. Instead of hat-in-hand humility, such seekers typically approach you as chummy counselors or assume an authoritative strut, rolling out their sales pitches. They assure that you have some flaw or lack, and your only salvation lies in the solution they just happen to have right here. Yet whatever their mask, these competitors stand as desperate as any. For they know very well what too many of us have forgotten: you cannot be wholly owned without your consent.

Who are they? Let's categorize the competition according to what parts of you they seek.

Cash and Time Requesters ∽ These come as commercials, ads in all media, and friendly tips/persuasions from unknown folks. Enticingly, you are asked to put their beer in your tummy, their chip in your computer, their couch in your living room, or their deodorant under your arms. Coupled with these seducers swarm the donor seekers. Come work at my soup kitchen. Send money to save these giant tortoises, save the city of Jerusalem for our kind of people, continue stem cell research, or support our veterans.

Each by each, such solicitations are relatively harmless and easily dismissed. Some may even inform you of benefits. You may find real gratification in supporting the local symphony, and applying that deodorant just might remove the obstacle to a new romance. The danger lies in the inundating volume of these advertisements and the festering insecurities they breed. You need a personal stylist to put a spin on your lackluster self. You are not nearly slender enough, fit enough, dressed attractively, or smart enough to gain admittance into that grand party of the successful that everyone but you seems to be enjoying. If you constantly are fending off this litany of inadequacies, you may subtly be drawn into doubts about your abilities and choices.

The power of these massed, persuasive solicitations stands evident in the wave of obsessive purchasing and the resulting endless debt that has gripped our culture. Too many of us define ourselves through the things we own. Unthinkingly, we begin to adopt the contemptuous label given us by these beggars: a consumer. As self-governing CEO, you will, of course, find far more appropriate ways to define Your Marvelous Self.

Elusive Image Peddlers ∾ To be what they desire you to be – that is their quest. These image sculptors seek more than your time or cash. They want your earnest belief in a prefabricated box of values. All those attributes bundled into the enviable image have been carefully sorted beforehand. And, most seductively, they are characteristics many of us already want for ourselves.

In the 1960s, *Playboy* magazine flooded the market and young men's minds with the burning question, "What Sort of Man Reads *Playboy*?" Hordes of centerfold-hungry males gobbled up Mr. Hefner's answer, acquiring all the knowledge of stereos, well-mixed drinks, art, dress, and masculine style *Playboy's* civilized hero embraced. The ascot and pipe made the devotees of this image easy to spot. But that's history and hindsight. How adept are you at spotting the enviable images of your own era?

The heroine strides across the screen into our view. We learn quickly that she is highly educated, vegan, erudite, and alluring without obvious effort. Her expertise is admired by all, and (very trendy) she can handle herself physically in any battle against males, females, or transgenders. Not a bad role model, actually. Yet, do you need to buy the entire package? Is this hero's "new shag" haircut or love of collard greens going to serve you any better than Hef's ascot and pipe? As CEO it becomes your job to tease apart adaptable abilities from unusable window dressing.

In the USA, it is autos. Cars are the vehicles carrying conscientiously crafted images that mold human to machine. When your computer-selected date drives up for that first meeting in a Volvo, Prius, Jeep, Lamborghini, Ford truck, or Mini Cooper, you've got him judged. Before he disembarks from the car, you've estimated his income, stance on social issues, presidential voting preferences, his plans for your first afternoon together, and pretty good odds on whether there will be a second meeting – or not. Regardless of your pre-judgments' accuracy, each of these guestimations has been deliberately packaged and planted by the manufacturer's marketing team. Love, the hippie-boomer generation was told, is what makes a Subaru a Subaru. And very cleverly, this maker has matched its design to the needs of this aging target market. Starting out as a lean, thrifty, venturesome vehicle in the 1970s, the Subaru, like its boomer-buyers, has gained in girth and padding and is now ample enough for all the grandkids. Such enviable ideals evolve, but they ever remain, dangled before us.

Like those seeking your fiscal and physical resources, image peddlers saturate every fiber of our cultural fabric. Business media never tires of romantically profiling gumption-based entrepreneurs who have risen from shoe string to billion dollar buyouts. Boy Scouts, universities, athletics – every force within our culture sets forth its own brand of hero – that ideal image for us to follow.

This hero market boasts a prehistoric pedigree. Ancient Greeks once defined their actions based on whether they followed the brutishly powerful Hercules or the ruthlessly cunning Theseus. Today, the problem with such hero-packages is the quiet subtlety of presentation. In fact, many role models are not hard-pitched sales jobs, but are completely inadvertent. The adventure-story author is not seeking benefit from our adopting the trappings of his fictionalized detective. Such authors merely gather a cohesive collection of admirable attributes into their character to make their work exciting.

Broccoli Moment Determine your heroes – those role models you actually follow. Think back on challenges in your past year and your preferred responses. Who guided those responses? Who was your role model? Now the tough one: what parts of that hero do you really want to keep on your mental board of advisors? Can you, as CEO, diagnose what aspects of these envisioned heroes serve you well?

Soul Solicitors ∾ Not some or most, the soul seeker wants all of you. He covets your every belief, effort, and thought. And he sets you on a faith track in which you yield up not only present, but all future judgments. In short, soul solicitors want to capture your devotion. The three most prominent soul seekers in most cultures are institutions of religious faith, your nation, and the company that employs you. Of course, others abound.

In each case, the institution's evangelical recruiters set before you a prix fixe menu with beliefs for every situation and tasks to fill your every moment. All choices have been made. All values, principles, and goals are laid out before you. As the old hymn goes, "Take thou my will, Oh God, and make it thine own." And wrapping up the package comes a gleaming legion of heroes, many of whom have given the last full measure of devotion for the cause: workaholic, martyr, bullet-riddled patriot.

Devotion to the soul solicitor involves a servitude-for-salvation swap. You surrender your precious personal will and judgment, along with a goodly amount of your time and resources. In return, you receive the promise of immediate and future salvation. When Jerry Falwell Jr., president of the conservative Christian Liberty University, suggested that faculty and students wear weapons as a warning to the Islamic threat, many complied. Upon being interviewed, several armed students claimed to have been unaware of an immediate Islamic threat but cited their faithful devotion to their religious principles as ample rationale for their action.

The true danger of the soul solicitor lies not in the creed, but in the surrender. A planet without the loving deeds inspired by our religions, for example, would be a terrifying world indeed. Yet even in this culture of caring intention, forsaking one's principles of personal judgment can send individuals down horribly unprincipled pathways. Sadly, mindless religious fanatics and patriots may commit acts that destroy themselves and ruin others. Then, why in heaven's sweet name would any self-governing person surrender himself so completely? Simply, because the compensations offered are so irresistibly enticing.

Those seeking your utmost devotion know how to wrap the package in ways that trigger your every hope and fulfillment. The actual truth – that your devotion is sought to help fuel the agenda of someone other than you – is, well, rather unsalable. The unvarnished display of an institution's self interest just does not offer you enough to inspire your enlisting. For example:

▶ Your employer knows he can scarcely hope to rally his workers under the motto of, "Let's fill the company coffers." So he tailors his compensations to his employees' individual goals. Those devoted to their employer take home the promise of tangible cash and intangible status. For the right position, perks include being envied, contributing to society, and perhaps a chance to scratch one's creative itch.

▶ Likewise, no temple ever pitches, "Put your faith in Buddha because we really need the followers." Instead, religions promise serenity, answers to cosmological questions, and the security that you are on track. You are no longer a wrench being used as a hammer; you are living the way you were divinely designed to live.

- Your nation's leaders will never ask you to "Love and die for your country because the folks in charge really crave the power and bucks." However accurate, this slogan holds slender appeal. Rather, those devoted to their country are assured security, along with a source of pride in protecting a worthwhile cause/leader.

- In the same vein, devotion to the Lakers Basketball team promises – well, no one's quite figured that one out yet.

Additionally, all of these institutions (even the Lakers) offer high placement on the acceptance scale:

The human herd is a vast and often lonely place. Finding that special niche where you are adopted by your fellows, your own self approved, and your deeds recognized – even celebrated, well, that's salvation. Any institution promising that is holding out the second-greatest fulfillment we *Homo sapiens* can wish for.

Individual Solicitors ∿ This person may be your bride, friend, hiking partner, fellow club member, or coworker. We list these acquaintances among your competitors because each of them has plans for your time and resources. And, though perhaps inadvertently, they do influence your choices with their own examples and advice.

As with all the beggars at your door, their intent is irrelevant. This kindly friend may truly want her vision of what is the very best and happiest for you. It matters not because only you possess the authoritative expertise on what is best for you. You are the go-to girl or guy for determining your own best interest. Only you know where their shoe pinches you.

CEO of Yourself

Your Competitive Advantage

To the individual seeking to blaze his own path and govern life with his own choices, these competitors seem fierce and relentless. They are. But you are the chief executive officer and the competition is not your enemy. As Laureate Biopharmaceutical's CEO Mike Griffith is fond of saying, "Competitors are only those who have not had the opportunity to learn how they may profitably partner with you, at a junior level."

Envision each competing solicitor for your goals and resources as an obsequious waiter bearing a dessert cart from which you may select at your leisure. Now is the time to explore what the various items have to offer. Look for the benefits. Resist the tendency to mount a me-vs.-them defense against the these peddlers. Do not concentrate on the obscene profits that might be harvested by the chef or the annoying urges of the waiter. See the cart merely for what it is, an array of offerings. And don't forget: you need not swallow any entire pie – ask for a sliver of the apple, the blueberry, and the cherry. Remember, you're the CEO.

Meanwhile, the avalanche of solicitations keep coming and will doubtless require a mental defense that allows you to clear your mind and get on with business. As an exercise, it may help to periodically restate your chosen principles and goals – out loud, boldly – to rechart your mind on its course. Secondly, restate your awareness that, however many and powerful, these solicitors are only beggars at your door, seeking a consent that you alone can give.

Yes, you are part of the human herd, and we humans are innately suggestible. You may unthinkingly be lulled into purchasing a set of steak knives on late night TV. But your strong, basic beliefs will kick in and nix any suggestion that you use them to carve up the cat. The more muscular your personal principles, the easier it becomes to ridicule these persuasions and seize only those elements that will make you the champion you seek to be.

The Ultimate Distraction

Earlier, we noted that soul solicitors' promise of high placement on the acceptance scale was the second-best salvation that can be tantalized before a person. So what's in first place? Almost nothing will make you as happy as to be drenched in the bliss of intimacy, romance, and love.

It feels fabulous, exciting, and fun. And it can last a lifetime. In fact, that whole mixed pot embracing sexual thrill, the rapture of adoration, and the deep abiding pleasure of sharing mutual love is just plain unbeatable.

None of these beggars seeking to lure your devotion can proffer any reward that can compete with it. And they know it. And it scares them more than a Christian Scientist with appendicitis. Love, romance, and intimacy provide the ultimate distraction from the plans soul seekers have painstakingly lined up for you. In real life, women toss away enviable careers for that beloved one they want to spend their lives with. Kings cast aside their crowns to marry the women they love.

So to keep us in line, societal sages claim that those smitten with love "have lost control," when in truth the only control lost is that of society over them. Love makes you go your own way – make choices that bring you happiness – and lets loose emotions that bring unrivaled fulfillment.

As love grows, the poor soul-soliciting institutions loose their handle on you. As you refuse to be steered toward their direction, their only hopes lie in law and propaganda. In the ancient Shona kingdom of what is now Zimbabwe, those men engaged in the holy, near-mystical art of making iron were forbidden to be in the company of wives or other women for a week prior to the work. Following that tradition, today's employers set laws forbidding intimacy, even dating, among fellows sharing the same place of work. Patriotic soldiers are warned that when it comes to fraternization, both sides are the enemy. Faith institutions handle the love threat with a bit more finesse. Constructing legions of religious intimacy strictures, their leaders cleverly try to convince you that properly sanitized love is their divinity's gift to you.

For the CEO of one's self, such institutional conniving shines as a beacon of warning. Any group that seeks to redirect, stifle, or condemn your love life is suspect. Their interests lie far apart from yours. Any role model that demands you sacrifice your love, intimacy, and romance for its salvation is offering you a false choice and is unworthy of your devotion. Intimacy haters are the weaklings of the solicitors. Laugh them to the scorn they deserve.

Finally, if you agree with some, but not all of the assessments put forth in this chapter, you are showing yourself to be a thoughtful, self-governing chief executive officer. Good for you. ▣

Afterthought ◌

The sardonically smiling Ambrose Bierce (1842 – 1914) spent the greater parts of his life as an itinerant journalist, humorously laying bare the naked truth about our bizarre human condition. Traveling and acting as editor for some of the noted periodicals in San Francisco, Washington, and England, he gained great fame as a writer of surprise-twist stories and articles that punctured the pompous. His culminating book, originally titled A Cynic's Discourse, earned him the nickname of Bitter Bierce. It was an instant hit and was soon retitled as The Devil's Dictionary. The definitions in this wincingly insightful volume remain a source of truth and laughter to this day. For example:

Bore: a person who talks when you wish him to listen.
Cynic: a blackguard whose faulty vision sees things as they are, not as they ought to be.
Habit: a shackle for the free.
Labor: one of the processes by which A acquires property for B.
Marriage: a community consisting of a master, a mistress, and two slaves, making in all, two.
Lawsuit: a machine which you go into as a pig, and come out as a sausage.
Prejudice: a vagrant opinion without any visible means of support.

Probably the best defense against the onslaughts of soliciting beggars grasping after your soul is to chuckle your way through The Devil's Dictionary and then exercise your dormant wit by developing a few definitions on your own. How would your marvelous self define texting, political party, employee motivators, and social media?

CEO of Yourself

Chapter 5

CEO Attitude Adjustments

*I don't care
if you've been COO for a decade,
when you become CEO,
your whole way of thinking and
acting changes. It has to.*

– George Wurtz, founding CEO of Soundview Paper

'Tis a simple but often painful truth. Great undertakings can be driven to fruition only by great attitudes. The high-gear shift from default mode to CEO of Your Marvelous Self involves more than merely doing things differently. The changes must go deeper – into the very core of your being and beliefs. Old comfortable attitudes and worldviews must be abandoned. More appropriate convictions that will effectively chart your new course must be adopted.

The broccoli moment demanded here is that attitudes may not be shed like last season's fashions. Your outlooks and the emotional responses they trigger have been hammer-forged on the anvil of your daily experience. An exhaustive and honest assessment is required. But once you can make these attitude shifts, the world opens before you like an oyster.

Myths and Mastery: Off with the Old

Forget the shrouded mists of ages past: Odysseus battling the Cyclops, George Washington cutting down the cherry tree, or Elvis still walking among us. Myths are commonly held beliefs. Every culture has them. They are pieces of the common lore that folks generally assume without much questioning. It is "well known" that:

▶ Hard work deserves good rewards.
▶ Science provides the best solutions to medical problems and most accurate answers to cosmological questions.
▶ You owe your nation allegiance.

Are these accepted beliefs true? False? Partially true? Much more to the point, how did you arrive at your opinion of these statements? In my own case, from my youngest days, I was continually instructed over and over and over that hard work and science were the answers to just about anything coming my way. And, with hand over heart, I daily pledged allegiance to my country, even before I understood what "allegiance" meant.

Most people encounter and absorb such myths within their cultural experience. Readily, we agree that the hardest laboring individual should get the promotion, top grade, or the big bucks. The person born, for example, in France who aids the German government at the expense his fellow French citizens earns not only the scorn of those in his native land but will be disdained by Chinese, Canadians, and people around the globe who hear of his actions. He is a betrayer – a Benedict Arnold who should join Judas Iscariot and be cast into the deepest circles of hell.

Unlike the solicited messages discussed in the previous chapter, myths seldom have a single source. They are carried among us by many messengers, most of whom seek no advantage or recognition for passing them on. This makes a myth truly difficult to spot. They are not presented to us for consideration. They just are.

So who cares? What's the problem with believing what I believe? The problem is that myths put your mind into default mode and thus limit creative thought. At a conference hosted by astrophysicist Neil deGrasse Tyson, a score of physics' best and brightest were ardently debating the issue of whether our current mathematics provide adequate tools for expanding our understanding of the universe. As a woefully under-educated journalist reporting on the conference, I posed my own innocent question: What if mathematics is not the sole tool for better understanding our universe? Are we willing to accept some other epistemological tool if it presents itself? The question and the ignorant journalist were summarily dismissed. Every expert in the room knew that mathematics was the sole and right tool. They believed this myth as surely as 16th-century Elizabethans believed that music was generated by the rotation of celestial spheres. These learned ladies and gentlemen were probably correct. Certainly I offered no better solution. But maybe, just maybe, some innovative physicist desperately seeking greater knowledge, like martial artist Bruce Lee ever searching for new methods, will not want to limit herself to the beliefs we all hold to be true today.

As CEO of Yourself, continually formulating your own principles for enriching your life, you will want to ferret out the generally accepted myths from the oceans of information flowing through your culture. You'll want to hold them up to the light of your own scrutiny. As a base starting point, examine the following two time-honored, globally accepted myths, and craft your own conclusions.

The Altruism Myth ∾

Helping others is a good thing. In fact, it is a better way to spend time than helping yourself. Believers in this myth, and they are the vast majority, are guided by the following:

▶ It is better for you to do something that helps someone else than helps yourself. Bill and former wife Melinda Gates are much more lauded for their charitable foundation than their $123 million house.

▶ The greater the sacrifice you make helping others, the more noble the deed and the more noble you are. Billionaire Mark Zuckerberg's gift of $100 million to the Newark school system won him far less applause than the widow whose charity cuts into her food budget or the avid football fan who sacrifices his Super Bowl tickets as a gift to disabled children.

▶ People whose primary aim is the helping of others are the most noble, happy, and wisest of individuals.

▶ Codicil: It does not matter a fig whom you help or how. Just so long as you serve someone who provides nothing in return.

Whether altruism is true or not, we all pay it lip service. We don't dare not to. People who openly announce, "The public be damned" receive instant condemnation. When railroad tycoon Cornelius Vanderbuilt spoke this phrase, it hit the headlines, and both his literal and metaphorical stock plummeted. Meanwhile, was Commodore Vanderbuilt, along with the reporter who quoted him, and every reader of that quote, all watching out for number one first? You bet your life. We all quite naturally put our happiness and well-being first, but most all of us openly profess the nobility of giving.

Beggars at Your Door

Altruism's supporters are legion: houses of faith, schools, governments (think tax deductions), and all groups who feel a responsibility for the entire cultural herd. Even self-centering Buddhism places at the top of its enlightenment scale those bodhisattvas who delay their own nirvana because they are compassionately moved to help other suffering beings along the path. Altruistic deeds promote primarily herd maintenance. The greatest good comes from serving the greatest number of our human herd. But what about the giver? Can he claim any benefit beyond praise? Is it worthwhile to strap on a giving and sharing nature as one element of your character? As CEO of Yourself, the answer lies within you. Yet, with so many people throughout all the ages announcing countless rewards from altruistic giving, if you haven't tried it, it might be worth experimenting a bit.

The Worth of Wealth ∾

The wealth each person achieves accurately reflects her/his worth as a person. Or so goes this mythic belief. Just the opposite of the altruism myth, virtually everyone publically denies this one but nonetheless clings to it, at least a little, in his heart.

Carlos Roderiguez, CEO of the payroll accounting company ADP, announced, "We hold the paycheck information of over 500,000 people, and it doesn't get any more sensitive than that." What is so sensitive about pay? People who happily share the full-color, close-up video of their latest child emerging from the womb would be offended if you asked how much money they make a year. We want to keep this exterior judgment of our worth as very private, like some dirty little fantasy that would cause death by embarrassment if publically disclosed.

Ironically, very few people believe that their compensation accurately reflects their contribution at work. The high-iron worker who returns home exhausted from erecting a skyscraper and the school teacher who has labored to open the wonderland of reading to a youngster, they know. Each understands that the supposedly super model who merely struts a runway for thousands per hour can't hold a candle to their contribution. But they value, and even en$, this gaunt-cheeked clothes horse due to her exponentially greater earnings. Given the choice, most teachers would rather share an evening basking in the reflected glow of a runway model than relaxing with their fellow educators.

CEO of Yourself

Even those who pull down the huge salaries feel this myth's grasp. Emma Watson who earned $60 million playing the role of Hermoine Granger in the Harry Potter film series expresses the fear that, "Someone is going to find out that I am a total fraud and don't deserve what I've achieved." If Emma had garnered $15 per hour for her days on the movie set, doubtless her anxieties would diminish considerably.

To this insidious myth countless thousands sacrifice their serenity. The financial broker who bounds gleefully into the house bearing a $50,000 year-end bonus will feel his spirit plummet upon learning that a coworker received $65,000. The Devil lies in comparisons. The fact that high cheekbones receive greater financial appreciation than high intelligence is a fleeting fact – at least today, at least in this culture. So it goes. It is natural to compare and measure. Yet this distraction of buying into other people's estimation of your worth will keep you, as CEO, from enjoying your current triumphs and laying the groundwork for future ones.

Myth Quiz

Take a look at these commonly held beliefs. Instead of puzzling over their accuracy, answer honestly: on a scale of 1 (not at all) to 5 (very much), to what extent do these cultural myths guide your actions and decisions?

- You have to be tough, even ruthless, to get ahead.
- All people are created equal. The successful deserve their success.
- Power corrupts. All those in positions of power are suspect.
- Time is of the essence.
- Education leads to a better and more rewarding career.
- It is better to innovate than to endure.
- You cannot be too careful nowadays.
- *Homo sapiens* are the highest life form on this planet. We are earth's stewards.
- Love is the most important force and greatest goal in life.
- I can be anything I want to be, do anything I set my mind to.
- People respond better when you give them respect.

Extra Credit: Name three commonly held myths in your social realm that most folks around you take as fact. Give your opinion on them.

CEO State of Readiness: On with the New

It may seem almost impossible. Fending off the hard press of all the alluring persuaders and wrenching yourself free of those mythic beliefs that have been guiding you since childhood is a daunting task. The good news lies in the fiery excitement accompanying the new convictions and attitudes you as CEO of Yourself will usher into your life.

Look within. You are tougher than you think. Attitude adjustments to your leadership must be made. And you are more than ready to take these beneficial perspectives listed below.

Wants vs. Shoulds and Gottas You do not want to be a slave to your goals. You know people like this. Every activity is a chore to be worked through. Be it scrubbing the kitchen floor or celebrating a friend's birthday with a wine tasting, it all goes on the sacred to-do list – one more task to be accomplished and endured. Life becomes a series of hurdles set daily before such folks by some exterior hand. Discipline and work ethic replace desire as the driving force. Ugh. This grim life seems scarcely worth living.

The entire purpose of taking the CEO's mastery of yourself is to fill your life with days of joyous enthusiasms. Of course, not every activity of every moment will imbue your heart with blissful rapture. Labor pains accompany each treasured birth. Yet joy or drudgery lies less in the deed of the moment than in the feeling that you freely attribute to it. With a little personal vision, you can reverse the shoulds and obligations into projects you anxiously undertake. The kitchen floor may be joyfully scrubbed in anticipation of a coming guest. That wearying fatigue that results from physical chores such as athletic training may fade from mind, as the power surge of accomplishment and thrill of straining to the utmost draw your attention. Just look at you lifting 20 more pounds than last week.

Asking Why Not? "There are no rules! We're trying to invent something here," yelled an enraged Thomas Edison at his nitpicking clerk. And so are you. Let life be an inviting avenue, not a maze strewn with official traffic lights and logistical limits. Concentrate on the freedoms, not the walls. Center your mind on a course that delights you and engineer a way to garner the most out of it.

Easy advice to give, but tough to follow. As we become herded into our crowded society, there lurks a tendency to get overwhelmed by the authorities and their rules. Subtly, slowly, we absorb the belief that every action requires a permission. Says who? 'Tis time to shatter that restrictive mindset. Scrutinize these permissions. Odds are excellent that most of them are conjured or amplified by your own imaginings, rather than some real and present authority.

One caveat here. After you have defiantly asked, "Why not?" pause a moment and ask, "Why?" Suddenly this morning, before rising, you are stricken by a desire to go explore Tasmania. Great idea. Probably. As CEO, you not only select the program, you have to determine how it fits into your overall vision and how it may be best manuevered. So before packing your pith helmet, you might consider asking: am I really enchanted with Tasmania, or am I merely seeking an escape from a loathsome life situation or a maritally hungry fiancé? And if it truly is to be Tasmania, don't forget to don your CEO backpack and plan the trek's ideal season, transport, and company.

Getting Emotive Choosing to become CEO of Yourself demands the greatest emotional commitment of your life. Each of us wants what we want with a passion. No need to coax this passion; it already lies waiting within. All it takes is for you to roll up your sleeves and tear down the walls of doubt. Then, with childlike innocence your emotional anticipation will stride out energizing your every endeavor.

Becoming Self-Centered Copernicus was correct. The world and all celestial bodies do not revolve around you. No one is suggesting that you establish yourself as a universal center around which all others must orbit. Yet, once you accept the reality that your vision, actions, and decisions sculpt your life, it only makes sense to concentrate on that initial rainmaker: You. Every effective CEO is constantly concerned with strengthening this prime generating asset. You may not be able to change the attitudes and acts of others, but your unrivaled self-mastery allows you to reinforce your own performance. So set your mind to it.

Even if your selected vision is to give all of yourself to enrich humankind, you still want to concentrate on donating the best gift possible. Concentrating on your own value need not make you self-absorbed. Rather, donning the mantle of CEO of Yourself means you merely realize the importance of your abilities in your own life.

Beggars at Your Door

Landmarks

New actions of self-decision and self-governance taste sweet and encourage sweeter attitudes. One bite of mastery increases the appetite for more. How do you tell if your chief executive is leading you along the right track? Monitor and watch your attitudes evolve as you grow more:

- **Eager** – I feel anxious for the next day and next adventure.

- **Principled** – My life has a moral compass governed by principles I have shaped and emotionally believe.

- **Active** – I'm not frenetically busy, but I'm more energetically engaged in the sumptuous feast of life.

- **Interested and Inquisitive** – That new optimism instills the feeling that something strange and new is also usually wonderful.

- **Fearless** – I still worry, but the desire to explore overwhelms that fear.

- **Stubborn** – No, I will not yield on my principles. Yes, I do want to persist on this unsure path for the sake of savoring the adventure and aiming for my goal.

- **Involved** – I've wholeheartedly plunged into the project at hand and simultaneously taken great interest in the folks and events all around.

On the other hand, beware false indicators. Not all attitudes held by folks we admire necessarily signify that they possess either the mastery or the happiness you seek. The demeanors listed below may be lovely and useful but are not required for engineering a bumptiously joyful ride through life.

- **Competent and Confident** – Some new and strange ventures make neither always possible. If you are always competent and confident, you're probably not exploring widely enough.

- **Intelligent** – 'Tis a helpful talent, although whimsically relative. It is seldom required and never a guarantee for achieving the life you seek.

- **Decisive** – A term typically applied to those whose decisions are rapid and immovable. Yet those unsure and slow to select may get there just the same.

CEO of Yourself

- **Sophisticated** – You mean like Albert Einstein?

- **Successful** – Triumphs are fleeting. Fortune favors those chief executive officers who manipulate the flow of circumstance as best they can. But outcomes lie in the fickle fingers of fate.

- **Ambitious** – If you yearn for rank and social advancement, you'll muddy your aim. If you crave accomplishment – go for it. ▣▣

Afterthought ∽

In 1837, former General and President Andrew Jackson died in his beloved Tennessee home, the Hermitage. He had fought against invading British soldiers, Indians, and political foes with fierceness that justified his nickname of Old Hickory. He had fought for American democracy with an energy and effectiveness that that few have ever matched, and he remade the American presidency into its modern role.

Learning of his death, one reporter traveled to the Hermitage and was greeted at the door by an old family servant. "Well what do you think," the reporter asked the lifelong retainer. "Do you think your master is going to heaven?" The other man scowled at the reporter a moment and, recalling Old Hickory's unconquerable demeanor, responded, "Well, who's gonna stop him?"

May the same be said of each of us.

CEO of Yourself

Chapter 6

Forging Your Own Principles

*Change your opinions,
keep to your principles; change your leaves,
keep intact your roots.*

– Victor Hugo

Life is messy. Life happens fast. People, events, persuasive ideas, and the IRS all juggernaut upon you at a pace that prevents pensive pondering. You simply don't have time to thoughtfully examine each new encounter, come to an informed decision, then carefully sculpt a reaction. As CEO of Yourself, you need a foundation for rapid response that still allows you to bring your best powers to bear on each situation and seize the results that fulfill your goals. Enter principles.

Creating personal principles affords you this rapid response platform. By principles, we mean those fundamental, proven beliefs that you have considered deeply, hold strongly in your heart, and employ as your life guide. For example:

▶ Free will is one of life's greatest gifts. Guard it well. Exercise it richly.

▶ My life is precious. I get only one shot at it. It serves me and others best if I use my time to create the greatest joy and fulfillment.

Principles provide both the riverbank and the river bottom as you flow through life. They add both direction and forward momentum to the current of your actions. The person who, for example, places a principal value on free will, will steer clear of organizations or career situations that would enslave his spirit. He will probably let his feet follow his imagination into strange fields and give a freer rein to the independent actions of his employees and children. Instinctively, he will bristle at the loss of liberty in others. Oppressive tyrants and seductive controllers enrage him. He may join a political party or even seek office to broaden others' free will. He may financially support civil liberties organizations and those battling for prison reform. All this wellspring of action, emotion, and thought surges from one fervently held principle.

Founding Fathers

In June 11, 1776, young Thomas Jefferson, charged by the Second Continental Congress, toiled over the wording of The Declaration of Independence. A true son of the Enlightenment, Jefferson dipped his quill in the inkwell and set down his own principle stating that people were "endowed by their Creator with certain inalienable Rights, that among these are Life, Liberty, and the pursuit of Happiness."

Upon reading it, the equally earnest Alexander Hamilton took objection. He wanted the words altered to say, "Life, Liberty, and the pursuit of Property."

Each man saw the threat of the English crown's incursions on the liberties of its colonials. Each wanted to defend what was most necessary to the fulfillment of the people, as he saw it. Emboldened by his principle, Thomas Jefferson went on to write and introduce the Virginia Statue for Religious Freedom, advocate for public education, as well as found the Library of Congress and the University of Virginia.

Hamilton, seeing the freedom to possess property as a greater avenue to personal power, became the architect for new America's economic system and advocated for national banks. He wrote most of the governmental-defining Federalist Papers and supported the incipient manufacturing might of the new nation.

Both of these founding fathers were guided and motivated by their differing principles. Both orchestrated an immense body of public service in accordance with their beliefs. Historically, you may consider which one was right. But today, it is far more vital to consider how you would finish the sentence: Among humankind's inalienable rights are...?

CEO of Yourself

Your Principle Platform

So, yes, you've doubtless gotten the message. The principles you craft are among the most important choices you make as a CEO of Yourself. You will lean on their support for future decisions. They will urge and direct you into lush new adventures. Slouching into default mode here will wreak havoc on all your future actions. It will set you hiking without a compass.* Certainly if anything is sacred in life, it is those governing beliefs that each of us holds dear, perhaps dearer than life itself.

Because of their very importance, all principles must be forged by *you* with the primary purpose of benefiting *you*. The only reason to hold a principle is that it fulfills you – that it brings you happiness. Of course, part of that happiness may include the joy of helping another or the prideful glow that you are making this globe a better place, but your principles must be self-formed and self-enriching.

This is a matter of efficiency, not morality. Principles adopted any other way and for any other reason simply will not work. Believing in an ideal because Dad, Christ, your commander-in-chief, or any external authority tells you so is a poor reason. We *Homo sapiens* make really unhappy slaves. We may fall in love with a particular authority temporarily. And we may willingly sacrifice our own desires in service of some larger or other good, for a while. But if this handed-down principle of self-governance brings no benefit to ourselves, in fairly short order we will turn away and reject the principle, or continue to adhere to it with an ever-seething resentment. Why govern yourself into misery?

As CEO of Yourself, you seek to build things that function and endure according to the principals you've set down. This means you want to think for yourself, but not entirely by yourself. Self-mastery does not exclude your seeking help, or shut your eyes to all the hard-wrought wisdom of the ages. As mentioned earlier, your house of faith, varied mentors, and innumerable organizations each holds out a prix-fixe menu of principles that they would simply adore you to unthinkingly swallow whole. These menus are not necessarily bad or good, nor are they irrelevant. They are fodder – standards for you to browse through and

---

A compass points the way to true north and lets you determine where you want to go. A GPS tells you where you currently are and provides you a route to somewhere else. We chose the more "old fashioned" instrument because the compass allows a freer individual choice and demands more work – just like being CEO of Yourself.

chew over. Those ideas you find particularly suitable may refine your current principles or even become candidates for new principles to be adopted.

Perhaps your experience is leading you to believe that a giving nature would bring you greater satisfaction and happiness. You might turn to biblical texts advocating the joy of generosity, e.g. loving your neighbor as your self; or that giving is an investment, e.g. – bread upon the waters – affording a ten-fold return in unexpected ways. Robert Greenleaf's essays on servant leadership may guide your considerations. And, of course, observing those you admire brings fuel to your thoughts. The governing principle you design, tempered by the lore of others, is still yours and still tailored to that unique you.

Broccoli Moment Does this mean you should actually write your personal principles down, like some sort of Gospel According to Me? Yes, exactly. For many readers, this exercise may prove less of a medicinal broccoli side dish and more of a refreshing sorbet.

On some evening when the air is cool, the breeze soft, and the night is very much yours alone, raise your eyes to the stars and think about what you believe. Jot down some fundamental truths as a foundation. Then, from these, try developing a few governing standards for your actions that would enrich you and all those around you. Be specific – this is a life-business plan you are calculating.

The goal of this contemplative evening is not to descend from the mountain with immutable, stone-etched commandments. Rather, let it be the first step. Your principles may be formed over time and reshaped at leisure so they might stand solid in the heat of battle. Save your writings. No need to share them; they are penned for you alone. Others will in time see your principles inscribed in your character.

To add a little structure to this thought process, consider the following path of how a raw idea becomes fashioned into a functioning principle.

Candidate Beliefs

Every belief starts out first as a candidate. It humbly knocks at your door. You review it and decide whether or not to let it in on a trial basis. If this belief stands up to your experience and scrutiny, with a little CEO reshaping, you may eventually bring it onboard as a guiding principle – a belief to live by and govern your actions.

For example, you ponder:

It seems like a good idea to give every person respect, to assume that all people are honorable characters, worthy of my consideration, perhaps even my compassion.

Many wise sages have preached this idea. You keep hearing it, so you turn it over in your mind:

Certainly, I see some benefits. This esteem given to others tends to be returned. And with this open attitude, I'd get to meet and understand a lot more people. That's a good thing. Besides, it makes me happier to approach folks that way. Hate and suspicion are such downers. Yes, this idea would be a real help to me.

But, you ask yourself, is it true:

Is everybody deserving of my respect? Lemme think....Yes, most of the people I've encountered have had something worthy of my admiration. Of course, there's that outrageous SOB in Accounting. He has no redeeming social value. And what about Joseph Stalin and Vlad the Impaler? I mean, I don't want to unthinkingly rubber stamp every creature I encounter as inherently admirable. A person needs to exercise her judgment.

So this belief that's drifted into your consideration receives a little sculpting. You rethink from that base belief:

All right. I believe in looking for and nurturing that admirable spark that lies in each person. Odds are good it will bring some benefit to me and to him. The world gets a little boost, and I get a happier outlook. No, I can't make each person my personal life's project, but just believing in that individual spark, with an eye toward compassion, will make my encounters a little richer.

With time, and the building of principles takes time, experience proves your belief as profitable, or not. In this case, approaching folks with respect for whatever good lies inside seems to bring what's promised. Even that SOB in Accounting, you discover, responds less nastily when treated with civility.

Of course, not every principle comes so laboriously wrought on the anvil of hea$ mental cogitation. Recently this author overheard two ladies at a very social party confiding. "Yeah, he's cute, but I never mess around with married men," said one. To which the other responded, "Oh I know what you mean. I just couldn't bear being the initiator of all that pain and bad feelings." Simple. Conclusion drawn; principle slipped into place; it's done. Actions get aligned with this belief, and both women are the happier for it.

Principles at Work

Remember, principles provide more of a grounding than mere directives. They inherently embrace both a belief and a resulting wise course of action that brings benefit. This is what makes principles very practical, very user-friendly tools. Not every belief offers guidance. Your conviction that either the world was divinely created in six days or that earth is the result of a more protracted, Darwinian evolution will not alter how you face the sunrise or your coworkers on the morrow.

Likewise there are other guiding sources that may help form principles but in themselves are incomplete. For example, goals are simply achievements aimed at: summiting Mount Everest, making your first million by age 28. They offer targets but no fulfilling guidance. Similarly, values comprise those ideals that you believe enrich you and/or the planet. But without bringing this ideal into the way you create yourself, they remain airy philosophic theories.

Blunders to Avoid Notice we have not even mentioned the term "mission." Yes, every solid business bases its products on a stated core mission. Employees have to understand why they are coming to work each day. So company founders come up with directional mission gems like:

▶ To become a dependable producer of more than 10 million tons of coal per annum. – *British Coal Company, Ltd.*

CEO of Yourself

- To make the tools that provide a cure for cancer. *– Ardent Healthcare*
- To become the world's leading provider of premium products and premium services for individual mobility. *– Bavarian Motor Works*

While all very noble and fiscally embellishing, such bronze-cast statements are far too confining for your life. Unlike a corporation, your spirit embraces far more than a single mission. Even those who decide to devote their lives to serving one deity perform that service through myriad, unrelated efforts. Instead of searching to distill your life into a lone, one-sentence purpose or single motivator, why not whip off the blinders? Develop a roster of guiding principles that will serve you in feasting on life's immensely varied banquet.

Experience will help you decide which principle platforms will set your life swiftly soaring upward. If you honestly believe that the world outside your door is nasty, brutish, and fraught with danger and that each new encounter demands your utmost aggressive posture, then follow your principle. It is yours, and for that reason worth acting upon. Just remember to review those principles for accuracy. Principles evolve with time. When the character you have produced fails in delivering the fulfillment you seek, 'tis time to tear apart those principles and bring on the repair kit.

One final caveat in structuring your personal principles: The key to wisdom is to never consider the source. Never, never validate any ideal or candidate belief based on the person or institution that first presented it to you. One day you read the solemn words, "I believe today that my conduct is in accordance with God Almighty." It sets a candidate belief in your mind:

> Perhaps I could find a richer happiness and make a greater contribution by living my life in accord with my Creator, as I perceive that divinity.

Then, amidst your considerations, you learn that these words were not, as you had thought, spoken by Jesus Christ during his crucifixion. Instead, they were proclaimed by Adolf Hitler before the German Reichstag.

Does it matter? The actions of the author add no weight to an idea's value. Whoever set this germ of an idea in your fertile mind is irrelevant. Mold each suggested thought to suit your chosen course and then employ it to help Your Marvelous Self take wing. **BB**

Forging Your Own Principles

Afterthought ∾

Chief Executive's Choice

Your good friend of over a decade has asked you for a substantial cash loan. He is honest, very well-intentioned, and he likes you a lot. He also has been just barely scraping by in his one-person business ever since you've been acquainted. You know the odds are slim that you will ever see any return of the "loan." Your friend will not starve, but his story convinces you that he really needs the money to avoid a major debt spiral. The amount for which he asks will definitely dent your savings but not impinge on your lifestyle.

Your pen pauses over your checkbook as you sit in private and consider:

Conventional wisdom agrees with Shakespeare's lines:

- *"Neither a borrower nor a lender be for loan oft' looses both self and friend."*
- *Your memory reminds you of the many good times you and your friend have shared, as well as the problems encountered from other folks' unrepaid loans.*
- *Your financial advisor adamantly suggests you follow Shakespeare's wisdom.*
- *Your father, if he knew, would verbosely warn you against it.*
- *Your spouse would support you either way but keep reminding you of all the problems your decision has launched.*
- *Your religion approves wholeheartedly and encourages you to make a gift of the money.*
- *Your emotional mind savors the potential gratification that would come from making the loan and from gaining an obligation.*
- *Your rational mind searches for various forms of sweat equity payback that would produce benefit from your generosity.*

Taking into account all this input, how would you, Mr./Ms. Self CEO, answer your friend's request? And more importantly – why?

Chapter 7

Your Product: Your Self

Yours is the world and all that's in it.
– Rudyard Kipling

Your principles will be the making of you. You are about to pour all those natural creative energies, that whole warehouse brim full of eager strengths and interests, into the swift course of your guiding principles. And they will set you toward your product: that enriched life you just know lies within your grasp. You have sought and engineered this product. No one deserves it more than you.

As noted before, your product – your desired life – is a combination of circumstance and the continuous stream of choices you make. And Fate is constantly changing course. Riches, good health, rank, accomplishment, thrilling love, each may dry up as the seasons alter your days. So rather than some fixed, envisioned existence, your real product must be the engine that delivers those better, fulfilling days: the masterful you. The self you want to be and the best possible life you construct, together become your product. Self and life get built from one process.

Character

Every product comprises two aspects:

What it is – its character
What it does for its user – its value.

An automobile is a tool for personal mobility. If it has been well produced with creative inventiveness and technical care, the car may lay claim to certain characteristic attributes: it may be a fast, safe, dependable tool of personal mobility. Springboarding from that character comes the automobile's value – what it can do for its owner. You, as the owner, may feel that this car affords me opportunities to visit a greater number of clients, thus gaining me wealth; opens new venues and experiences to me and my family; allows me to attend more activities, impress those I want to impress; makes me seem enviable and sexy; offers me privacy and freedom......and on and on.

So it goes with Your Marvelous Self. Your character is that special you-ness that marks and guides your behavior. It is an outgrowth of your real and ideal beliefs. For example, you may hold the principle of doing no unnecessary harm to living creatures. It is a principle you try to follow. Living by this concept develops an element of your character – you are kind. Bundled together with other principle-based elements, your character becomes formed. Henry is kind, fun-loving, generous, honest, intellectually curious, and physically energetic. However, if Henry takes a painfully honest look at his character, a little soul searching may also add fearful, fastidious, and uncertain.

Like the selected principles of the first list, the second ones also hang on principle. Experience may have led Henry to believe that failure always carries punishment. He may further operate on the principle that the world is massively bewildering and disorganized, and the only hope for finding success and approval lies in nailing down each little detail to the letter.

We don't talk much about character any more. Character seems to be one of those unfortunate babies that got tossed out with the bathwater of Victorianism. It is old-fashioned. Like a yellowed page of Kipling's poetry. Somehow, back then, developing character got mixed into that endless list of life rules that were handed down from fire-breathing prelates and stiff-bodied matriarchs, all designed to make us better and more obedient. Wisely, we rebelled against this system of dictates that gave equal value the fullness of one's skirt and the fullness of personal compassion. The problem is that most modern cultures have not replaced the Victorian version of character with much. Today we ignore what a person is, concentrating instead on his actions and psychological motivators.

This character de-emphasis affords the freedom to shape character your way. Henry can labor to alter his fearfulness without the whole burden of society constantly assuring him of failure's many punishments. Likewise, you may take a look at those weathered lists of character elements – endurance, iron resolve, individual courage, etc. – and, if you so choose, build them into your masterful product. Yes, you can indeed mold your own character.

Blunders to Avoid "None of my executives can ever make a decision without me," complained a business owner to leadership consultant Dr. Stephen G. Payne. "Well, Mr. CEO, how much of that problem are you willing to own?" responded Payne. After some questioning, Payne's CEO admitted that he often withheld information and kept his staff terrified. Without thinking, he cut people off when their opinions differed. Slowly, accepting his responsibility for his employees' actions, our CEO rose gratefully and pumped Payne's hand. He thanked him and promised to check himself in the future. He would share information and stop the denigrating remarks. "No you won't," replied Payne. "Not if you are counting on raw will power alone. You've got to dig deeper."

Like Payne's CEO, most folks seek to improve their character from the back end – by correcting their behavior. Though noble, 'tis a discipline bound for failure. It's like trying to kill a weed by pruning its flowers.

Instead of striving to battle a lifetime of instinct, why not root out those belief principles that trigger fear of criticism and fearful acts? How accurate is this CEO's belief that his entire staff stands poised to bring about his downfall? If he can lessen his expectation of attack, the fear will melt and open the way for a more desired character element to follow.

Who's on Your Board?

Your character develops from selecting models you admire along your journeys. Most of us carry around a mental boardroom filled with influential personalities. They may be individuals who consistently accomplish outcomes we yearn for, like Bill Gates, your favorite James Bond, my rich Uncle Salvatore who made it all on his own, or that pesky girl in high school who always got everyone's attention. They may be speakers whose words move us, such as the Buddha, Gloria Steinem, or Barack Obama. Still others get grandfathered in with tradition and a little societal insistence: Mom, Dad, that high school coach, or your workplace supervisor.

Whatever their qualifications, such figures rattle around in our heads, nudging or even dictating our decisions. It's a Frankensteinian process, really. We elect pieces of several individuals, envisioning them through the lens of our own perception. We give each his or her own voice and stitch them together into a unified, persuasive body. Sometimes we consult them. More often, their advice slips into our consciousness unbidden. We feel these chosen models reflect the character we want, or should want, so we listen.

Tips and Tasks These board seats are filled with mere chimeras. They are but your perception of their perceived judgments. In fact, the actual people you usher into your boardroom would probably be surprised at their membership. But the real key is that you have freely elected these members. Every one serves at your pleasure. And while each one is influential, they are not necessarily beneficial. They exist, as does any board, to keep you true to your principles and to guide you in getting the wherewithal to fulfill your missions. So when you tire of the destructive advice opined by that pesky high school rival, fire her. You mentally brought her on – so reach into your psyche and make the CEO decision, "I need not be governed by my perception of Mary Beth anymore."

In the end, each of us cobbles together a character that is part real, part ideal. Those real attributes that define us, join with those ideal elements that bring us closer to that person we want to be. Most often, building your character into a better product is less a matter of replacing elements than enhancing dormant qualities that already lie within. Recalling our previous character example, Henry may still remain fun-loving and enthusiastically curious, as his experienced-based principles have proved advantageous; but he may also strive to, in the poet's words:

> meet Triumph and Disaster
> And treat those two impostors just the same.

If he can, he may make of himself a better fulfillment engine – an improved CEO, more able to seize the world and all that's in it.

A little construction note: As you strive to build that more ideal character, you are bound to make missteps. You will fail to deliver on some elements you're working towards. You will disappoint yourself, violate your own personal code, and in your own eyes, you'll have sinned. If you don't have a solid forgiveness system set into place, you may burden yourself with a hea$ knapsack of regrets. Hopefully you are the kind of CEO who can refocus on your many positive aspects, add a dash of understanding, and rebuild practical solutions for a better next quarter.

CEO of Yourself

Springboard to Value

No logical line leads straight from character to value. Just because the CEO designed it as a screwdriver does not prevent the client from employing it as a very valued can opener. Any automotive maker might well scratch his head trying to figure how horsepower, in the hands of a client, translates into sex appeal. But then again, that's not really his concern. If the client finds automotive enrichment from the mighty roar of an overpowered engine, well, put away the Freud and pull down the copy of Competition Engine Building.

Value is where the seemingly philosophic examinations of principles and character hit the hard reality of practical use. Character is merely potential. It's your state of readiness standing poised to seize every advantage fate sends your way. The value (or for those preferring business terminology, the value proposition) of this character lies in how well it brings you closer to that richer experience that you know is out there. You have restructured your character. You have shaken up and tightened up your board of directors. You've constructed a new, improved platform, but are you building the right tool for the jobs you want done?

Remember your initial wants? You want to:

▶ Wake up happy.
▶ Gain some real appreciation, uncalculated praise, or honest influence over others.
▶ Find some true back-slapping buddies.
▶ Lead an adventurous life; maybe do some high-altitude climbing in Tibet.

Is this character you're building designed to steer you toward these valued goals? Or might you be so busy tending and disciplining yourself for these new character elements that your fulfillment drifts into the background? You may have chiseled a character that embodies the traits of tenacious persistence and a newly less-fearful boldness. Good for you. But how is the value playing out? Perhaps your bolder manner may work toward the life upgrade of greater influence and reaching out to more friendly folks. Perhaps the process of developing persistence has boosted your esteem in your eyes and those of your friends as well. It may also have fired your courage to prepare for that Tibetan trek.

Or maybe, the bolder you is merely an ideal you pulled off someone else's shelf. And it's not leading you anywhere. Our mortal span on this globe is short. Make sure the value and experiences you require are getting answered by your product. As Self CEO, remember to review your goals and sharpen first those tools of character that will bring them to you. An ideal is worth shooting at only if it brings down the game you truly want to take home.

Reputation

"Who steals my purse steals trash....but he that filches from me my good name....makes me poor indeed."

These oft-quoted words from Shakespeare's play *Othello* still ring down through the ages. Yet with all due respect to the Immortal Bard, let's pause and take a good look at the value of what's being filched here. Your reputation is basically your character as seen through the eyes of others. Viewed this way, a solid reputation is a treasured tool. You will be given plum assignments and an upward path of greater opportunities as long as influential people hold you in high repute.

If the sincere, compassionate, and generous elements of Valerie's character are noticed by others, she will have little problem gaining friends and popularity. Conversely, Matt may work like a demon, be scrupulously honest, and cleverly innovative at work, but if his coworkers somehow repute him as lazy and untrustworthy, poor Matt will remain poor indeed. It just makes sense for a Self CEO to make others aware of those many admirable assets in his character. A little honest self-selling, gently done, goes a long way – provided, of course, you can fulfill on each characteristic you market.

However, reputation used as a standard of measure is worse than trash. Taking others' evaluations as a guide will be your ruin. At best, it will send you off chasing rainbows of conceit, filling pots of gold for perceived opinions. At worst, it will lead you onto a spiral of self-loathing and self-destruction, possibly even suicide. Ever since Sophocles' play *Ajax* the theatre has been filled with such tragic tales.

Quite naturally, we all do lean toward our strengths as others point them out to us. Often as not these reported strengths are offered with no note of self-interest or malice. Friends and acquaintences of young Jason may comment:

- ▶ "Wow, my man, you're really strong."
- ▶ "You've really gotten muscular lately, Buddy."
- ▶ "Boy I saw those biceps Jason, and decided not to mess with you."

Yet if Jason takes these compliments to heart, he becomes an actor on the stage before others. He labors long hours at the gym and becomes a slave to the praises of those around him. In short, he forfeits his self-mastery.

So yes, devote some time to achieving that valuable reputation. And even revel briefly in spontaneous praise. 'Tis a heady nectar that when sipped periodically will entice you to higher esteem and achievement. But do not invite those outside voices onto your board of directors. Instead, set your sights on developing character you personally admire. Build the self you like first. Others will be surprisingly quick to provide you with the reflective reputation you have richly earned. ▣

Afterthought ∾

A 75-kilometers march across the desert with no water in sight. In the spring of 329 B.C. Alexander the Great led his troops across the scorching sands of the Bactrian desert which, historians record, heated both men an animals as if wrapped by perpetual fire. Alexander had sent scouts ahead to an oasis to find water. Later, the lead scout returned and stood before his general with the bad news: the oasis had dried up to a trickle. He held out a single helmet filled with water saying, "I have brought this back – just enough for you, my lord. It was all the water I could find."

Accepting the helmet filled with the precious liquid, Alexander held it aloft before his troops. Then slowly, he turned the helmet over and poured the water into the sand. "Until we all can drink, I shall not drink," the leader announced. The march continued. When at last the army reached the Oxus River, Alexander waited until all the whole train had taken its fill. Character is a matter of choice.

CEO of Yourself

My Thoughts...

A few thought starters, and
a little space to jot down
what's of value to remember.

The role models I most admire are..... except for his/her.....

The belief systems I'm most aligned with are....
except for their insistence on...

Five of my personal principles that I hold dear,
and that guide my actions are...
(Bonus: one principle I'm currently considering for my
principles candidate list is...)

The roster of my mental board of directors includes
A. These folks I want to keep
B. These clowns I really need to fire and
get out of my head... (see page 57)

CEO of Yourself

These words describe my character – who I am....
And these words describe my value to myself
and others...

Getting Down to Work

CEO of Yourself

Chapter 8

Emotions

They are the force that is always with you
– Robert Solomon

Spock is a loser, and so's his old man. Search the television oldies channels long enough, and you're bound to find the original *Star Trek* series portraying the endless exploratory journeys of the futuristic star ship *Enterprise* across the universe. Among its marvelously allegorical crew strides the undyingly popular and ever-parodied Spock, initially played by Leonard Nimoy. The character of Spock, by "virtue" of being half-Vulcan is a man innately possessing almost no emotions. As science officer and second-in-command, he acts as a foil to the emotionally driven Captain James Tiberius Kirk.

Spock's full-Vulcan father, Sarek, boasts of being completely devoid of emotions. For father and son, this genetically altered state is depicted as a wellspring of strength. In this fictional series, Vulcans, by replacing the pestilence of emotions with the icy fantasy of pure logic, have been able to rid their planet of war, pollution, stress, conflict, and presumably spaceship rage.

Forward warp 9 into the real world. We call Spock and Sarek losers because they are like a pole vaulter who cuts off his arm to save weight. Emotions are your way of dealing with the world as it flows at you. You'd be lost and ineffective without them. Your emotions are surprising, often conflicting, unquantifiable; and above all, they are the most powerful motivating resource we *Homo sapiens* hold in our arsenal. And what's most wonderful: they come into your life at your bidding. Yes, emotions are intentional.

For a brief moment, imagine an emotionless life. You would shift into neutral, a state tellingly labeled apathea by the ancient Greeks. Rather than striving for great moral creations, you'd become a disinterested, passionless zombie. You wouldn't start war, nor would you be sympathetically roused to protect those falling under its oppression. You would not pick up on the many signals given by your team at work that they are unmotivated and feel unappreciated. But you probably wouldn't care very much, since you would hold no passion for the business you had founded. Worst of all, you would completely miss out on that exhilarating joy that comes from playing and bumping around with other folks.

Your Emotive Process

Love. Grief. Anger. Guilt. Compassion. Disgust. Desire. Jealousy. Joy. Surprise. From where do all these amazing passions spring? They seem at best vaguely defined and less understood. Even the sacred authority of *Webster's Dictionary* makes the mistake of seizing only the middle piece of emotions, defining them as "an agitation, disturbance...a tumultuous departure from more settled homeostasis." Yet for the Self CEO, operating to construct a richer, happier life, there needs to be a deeper understanding of our emotive experience.

In the fullest sense, emotions are personal surges of judgment, spiritual motivation, and physical prowess, all responding to the events of this messy, bewildering world. Emotions comprise an ongoing personal force that instinctively:

▶ Assesses what's going on in a situation.
▶ Interprets this incident's value to you.
▶ Then motivates an action to this current opportunity/threat.

They are your Einstein, Freud, and John Wayne rolled into one.

A large, muscular stranger comes racing across the street at you, arm outstretched, with something dark in his hand. Emotions kick in. Instantly, all other parts of your environment dwindle, as all your fullest attention centers on this charging individual. Quickly your senses determine that physically you probably cannot defeat this man. Fear! Muscles tighten, blood pumps, you look for a place to flee. (Had your pursuer been a child, an entirely different threat evaluation would follow the assessment.) You sprint a few swift steps. The long building behind blocks all escape routes. Anger now storms to the fore, enhancing prowess. Who does this bozo think he is, threatening me with harm? I'll show him not to mess with me. Wrath. Fingers flex to fists. Facial muscles contort to a menacing scowl.

Then a rapid reinterpretation. That thing in his hand....Could that be mine? Then come the stranger's words, "Excuse me sir. I'm glad I caught you. You're really fast. This is your wallet. You dropped it back in the restaurant when you were paying at the counter." Relief. Embarrassment flushes in. I hope this guy didn't see me as fearful and suspicious. Gratitude. That was very kind of this stranger to run after me like that. I want to reward him. Generosity. As you walk away, you gaze at the setting sun and savor its great beauty. Boy, I don't think I've ever seen such a radiant sunset. Sense of the sublime.

This time, your emotions got it right. You reassessed and reinterpreted in time to avoid punching your good Samaritan in the mouth. Had the muscular stranger been a mugger, perhaps your assessment and emotional response would have filled you with the required strength to scramble up a nearby fire escape or tackle him thuddingly to earth. Either way, the necessary emotional tools set you in a state of response readiness.

Such is the surging of the emotional tide. Each emotive response centers your whole being to appraise, evaluate, act. Like any personal force at the CEO's command, these passions cannot be denied. Rather, as CEO you welcome, marshal, and direct them into the best position for optimal use. At least, that's the ideal. Most of us do not end up employing emotions profitably because of life-long instructions that reject our emotions' value and refuse to see them as a choice.

Emotions' Bad Rap

In Western culture, emotions have suffered a negative reputation dating back to ancient Greece's earliest seekers of truth. Aristotle and the philosophic band calling themselves Stoics separated each person's intelligence (pure Spockian reason) from his emotions, which they termed the passions, (Greek for suffering). This opposing-camps concept, fueled by fiery theological persuasions inspired millennia of anti-emotion attitudes. Western pundits have poured forth ceaseless diatribes outlining the destructiveness of fear, lust, greed, wrath, and all things passionate. We have been carefully taught to stop experiencing and feeling, and start reasoning. A parade of great minds such as John Stuart Mill, have earnestly assured us that if we would only think and act according to the plan they logically deemed best for us, we would have no need for our own emotions. Thus the Spockian, emotionless-ideal myth has been planted and nourished. Yet, as an aware Self CEO, you see this preachment for what it is: another person's behavior-mandate myth, hanging on in our culture by a long historical tale.

To be fair, our terrifyingly powerful passions are not without flaw. Emotions do not always get our view of the world right. They target the wrong objects, or they misinterpret the intent. They also fire off energetic, yet amazingly inappropriate, responses. You road-ragingly hammer on your horn, curse, and call into question the parentage of the driver in the car ahead of you, who is just as mired in the traffic jam as you are. Then, for good measure, you express to your son beside you the stupidity of his wanting to go to his little league baseball game in the first place, and you expand his vocabulary along unfortunate avenues.

Further, emotions are absolute. You are not equivocally miffed by this cussed traffic jam; you are wholeheartedly outraged. In fact, the only effective quelling of this emotion will probably come when you behold the shocked expression on your son's face, and you replace your anger with a cocktail of love, regret, shame, and parental hope. And that is where your CEO oversight comes into play.

Passion Management

You are not a slave to your emotions. Yes, it may feel sometimes that you have been smitten by love, fallen prey to anger, or woken up one morning possessed by jealousy. The assessment and evaluation have come so rapidly, and the ensuing action with such force, that you may have missed your intentional unleashing of these emotions. But indeed, 'twas you who let them loose.

Regardless of all this culture's emotophobic preachings, your emotive process is inspired and set into action by your will alone. Your emotions are not some unbidden physiological response, akin to a leg cramp, triggered so deep within your autonomic neural pathways that they are beyond personal control. Numerous schools of science seek to map the physiological cues coinciding with emotional arousal, hinting that the source of our emotions lies programmed in our genes, not in ourselves. However, your poor body could not possibly come up with a separate set of responses for each of the literally hundreds of emotions that you daily employ. And as Self CEO, beware of anyone assuring you that self-mastery stands beyond you. See it as the insult it is.

All right, your powerful emotions fall well within your oversight. Fine. How might you best channel them so they may drive you toward your enriched-life goal? How does this CEO best play with this rampaging personal fire? Since history's dawn, this question has puzzled and spawned more theories than one could ever list. In answer, let us apply the business method and review what has worked best for other executing officers.

Poet and philosopher Friedrich Nietzsche praises the self-mastery of anyone who has organized the chaos of his passions to bring style to his own character. Certainly, your emotions are unique. They are not fixed entities grabbed off the rack. Your compassion or sense of surprise custom fits your character alone.

Thus it behooves you, Mr. CEO, to labor at gaining some emotional awareness – part of what has been termed emotional intelligence. Sort though your own emotional repertoire. Try to tease out your most frequently used, most powerful, and most successfully employed emotions. Inventory your conflicting emotions toward a single object. Instead of waiting and passively seeing what slides down the emotional pipe, take a manager's approach. Learn what elements compose your emotional stance and determine how you may put them together for your greatest benefit.

Also, study your passionate expressions. Do these emotional responses reflect the principles and character you have crafted? The way you display them may be like the soft rumbling urgency of Winston Churchill or the raging outbursts of a rock star on stage. The expression hinges on your character alone. As Self CEO charged with seizing that richer life, allow your passions to be as honest and bold as the rest of you.

Tips and Tasks Take a look at your temperament. Are you chronically intense, angry, humorous? These emotional predispositions give insight into your soul, and more importantly they point to a lurking inflexibility. If you attack even a party game with utmost seriousness or find that most life changes inspire your ire or that moral oppression brings only a joke to mind, perhaps you are thwarting other honest emotions. You may have pushed certain emotional reactions into the first-response position, which may make you a less effective and certainly less happy person.

Emotions   73

Blunders to Avoid The goal is to make your emotions honest – not appropriate to public expectation. Expressions carefully manufactured and presented for effect are playacting. How useful is an outward expression of stoic calm when you are seething with indignation at some harmful moral impropriety?

Granted, culture plays its part. Society nudges and hems the expression of emotions, making some displays taboo and placing others onto the preferred list. Recently, American women have been encouraged to display outrage and anger as a long-denied right and as an effective avenue toward social achievement. As CEO you'll want to study such cultural offerings and see if any benefit comes from adopting them.

Your passions blossom within the world around you. Maintaining your emotional integrity on life's stage before an audience requires some balancing. As the passions-leery Aristotle in his *Rhetoric* suggests, wisdom consists of unleashing the right emotion at the right person, to the right degree, at the right time, for the right purpose, in the right way. Right on, Aristotle. Does that competitor's trying to steal your best marketer or flirt with your fiancée appropriately demand a clench-fisted retaliation, or might it be seen as a nonthreatening compliment?

Decisions, Decisions Back in Chapter 1, we noted that the first half of the chief executive officer's duties are to assess, create a vision, and decide on courses of action. All of these steps require your emotional input. It is impossible to make rational judgments without the aid of emotions. How can you effectively choose the meaning and value of any option without involving your feelings?

Suppose you seek a career move. The icy light of passionless reason may quantitatively guide you into an ideal position with the highest possible earnings-to-expenses ratio, the greatest comparative income surplus, the shortest workweek, and the least amount of company oversight. Congratulations. Your reason has just landed you a career as yak herder in northern Mongolia.

You simply cannot separate them: the rational decision includes your passionate evaluation. Knowing just how great is your desire, along with what you are willing to expend and risk to achieve it, gives your choice meaning.

CEO of Yourself

Emotionally Motivated The remaining three CEO duties – assembling resources, enlisting aid, and moving forward into execution – all benefit from emotional supercharging. And this supercharging motivates us in a surprisingly seductive way. When Romeo first spies Juliet, he spurs his courage to meet her by emotionally bestowing the lyrical superlative, "So shows a snowy dove trooping with crows, as yonder lady o'er her fellows shows." Throughout history, gentlemen and ladies have summoned such courage and sustained their own relationships by passionately lavishing idealized characteristics on their best beloveds. This writer included. From my first encounter with my own sweet bride, my emotions poured every desire and womanly ideal into this lady, and the spell has held. The romance still burns daily with a delightful ferocity that melts away arguments, banishes flaws, inspires poetry, and provides each shared moment with matchelss intensity. Beat that, Spock.

This emotional idealization is not entirely bad. All of us have labored to live up to the sincere depictions of those we admire and respect. I am the greater man for having my coach, my supervisor, my friend believe in me. Yet at some point, if you are managing your emotive response to be appropriate and effective, you must be careful to identify the layers of idealism before measuring out your action.

Celebration vs. Control

When it comes to your passions, we agree with the German idealist G.W.F. Hegel that life well lived is akin to a bacchanalian revel. Celebrate your emotions. Err on the side of giving them free rein. Inject your emotional power into your thought and actions. After all, the entire vision that you as CEO of Yourself are striving to bring about is an emotional state – one of both viewing and feeling. You want the joy of today and the poised readiness to seize the fulfilling happiness from tomorrow's flow of circumstance.

You will find legions in the opposing camp, anxious to advise you on controlling your emotions. Interestingly, the noted inner-analysis guru Daniel Goleman, who in the early 1990s popularized the term "emotional intelligence," ardently directed folks to control their passions. Like many before him, he sought to make the fire of passion acceptable only if it was continually staunched to an ember. Don't emote too freely, insisted Goleman – just squeeze it out in droplets.

Emotions

Currently, business-leadership sages have gotten into the act, designing tactics to shift from one emotion to another. Employing such techniques as re-representing, anchoring, and meditative focus, you may train yourself away from the emotions you do have toward the emotions they say you should have. These mind-bending techniques may remind you of those prudish priests who once taught youngsters to transform the energy of sexual arousal into pushups.

The problem with attempts to control, sit on, or transfer your honest emotions is that they simply cannot be sustained. They work only in the short run. We all have witnessed the unhappy results of those who bottle up their emotions. Further, for the Self CEO, denying emotions is a tragic waste. The entrepreneur seeking to make her venture thrive does not eek out her money, intellect, muscle, or other resources by the spoonful. So why let trepidations about your mysterious, wonderful passions deter you from unleashing them full blast?

Emotions Fire Action They are blind to possibilities – and sometimes a little intentional blindness is what it takes to win victories. Without the emotions of anger and wrath, you could not possess moral indignation. Colonists dedicated to serene resignation could not have brought forth the American Revolution and its ensuing democracy. Without lust, you could not magnify and imbue your best beloved with all those attributes that ever enrich your passionate celebration of each other.

Actually, most of us treasure our passions. But we fail to see them for the inestimable resource they really are. When you were wandering through your warehouse in Chapter 2, did you list your emotions as enhancing assets to Your Marvelous Self? If not, now is the time to count their potential. Of course, you will venture to guide your emotional repertoire into the most productive situations. Yet rather than approaching your passionate energies with only caution, perhaps you may want to blend in a little gratitude and exultation over these not-quite-comprehensible powers that have been dropped into your waiting hands. **BB**

Afterthought ❧

Harriet Tubman rose from the bushes, giving signal to the small band of escaping slaves making their way through the marsh to the rendezvous point. In the moonless night, she motioned them to halt and be silent. Harriet raised a pistol and thrust it inches from the face of the man who had led the group to her. "All of you," she said, "are going to face the most difficult journey of your lives. You will have to snake your way along rivers, follow the stars through wilderness at night, escape bounty hunters, and suffer more than you ever did on the plantation. If you want to be free, come with me. If you want to go back, let me know so I can shoot you now, and you will not jeopardize those with the courage to go on."

Harriet Tubman led over a dozen bands of escaped slaves along the underground railway to freedom. Each runaway slave had to conjure the emotional power to undertake this life-threatening journey. Individually, each escapee had to dig down and summon the emotional cocktail of fear, anger, courage, desire, ambition, and passion required to make this seemingly impossible sojourn. These freed people brought it forth. Can you summon the emotional power to drive you toward the star you seek?

Emotions

CEO of Yourself

Chapter 9

The Call of Career

Career is a basket constantly refilled with new ventures and new lines of work. –BJ

In the bad old days when fewer choices presented themselves, you would have called it "my trade." An honest appellation, it defined those precious hours of your life in which you offered up the skills and labors you did have in exchange for those things that you didn't have and dearly wanted. Farm worker, cabinetmaker, merchant, pedagogue, or whatever trade you professed, it was the means by which you got and got along in society.

It's good to remember that term because it reminds you of what you are really doing when you straighten your tie or tool belt and go off to work. And amidst all the added tedious frills of today's certification process, educational readiness, and job-hunting, your choice to enter into some contributing line of work still involves that basic exchange agreement.

Of course, you don't have to enter a trade. You can opt to be a gleaner or a bandit, scavenging others' stuff. You can marry in exchange for those things you dearly want. You may operate completely outside society, hunting and manufacturing what you want from our natural Eden. All are viable choices. But you will indeed labor. The ancient poet Homer talks of "the tyranny of the belly, to which all men are grumbling subjects." And even in this digital age, each of us must sacrifice time and effort when that most elemental tyrant hollers, "Feed me!" The good news is that many more exciting avenues may now be found to answer that call.

Nowadays, if you possess the time and ability to read these pages, you hold the opportunity to shape a completely individual career. As CEO of Yourself, you have already designed your life from the principles up. You are empowering it with your personal character and emotions. So why not explore and carve a few new paths from the traditional employment avenues?

The very word *career* springs from the Latin root for cart or vehicle. And once you tear down that cardboard wall separating your trade from your non-trade pursuits, you can spy many further and fruitful vistas toward which your well-chosen cart may carry you. For instance, why not expand your definition of career to cover any selected field or pursuit involving progressive achievement? And why not envision your career as contributing force, rather than the label of some particular labor?

Suddenly, more of you is brought into play. A wider span of your talents is called for. Also, a far greater range of traditional trades spring up, offering fulfillment of your career goals. Instead of saying you are a professional singer, you view yourself as providing people with enlightening entertainment – like Lady Gaga. Instead of being a computer and electrical engineer, you view yourself as "an agent to prolong civilization and minimize the probability of a dark age" – like Elon Musk, creator of Tesla, Solar City, SpaceX, and PayPal. Your world enlarges.

As radio host of *Trenton 365*, Jacque Howard started off in a career as community reporter, telling folks of the many underappreciated people and activities in New Jersey's capital city. Then somewhere into his shows, Jacque shifted his career from civic reporting to civic engagement. He set out to make his home city a richer, more cohesive community in which to live. From gathering volunteers for parks renovation and establishing library boxes, to political reform and arts celebrations, Jacque now feeds his single career goal in a life that, while frenzied, is increasingly fulfilling. Meanwhile, Howard's *Trenton 365* show has soared in popularity, with listeners from 70 countries tuning in to find out what fascinating ventures the folks in this faraway city are up to now.

Even within industry and commerce, the traditional job boxes are crumbling. The same desperately competitive business climate that is dismissing gender and ethnic hiring biases is leading to a more holistic search for talent. Companies want every skill and idea employees can produce. Yes, you may be brought on board to fill a single trade slot – marketer, cobbler, data specialist, chemical researcher, Indian chief – but employers seek more than just the shark's fin. They want the whole, thinking animal. New titles like solutions architect, growth/development engineer, and innovation chief, indicate that employers want you to hurl your entire marvelous self into the game. "You're hired, son," they're saying. "Show us everything you've got."

Blunders to Avoid Beware of letting your career define you. Alas, this whole-soul approach adopted by corporations does not extend throughout society. Be honest now. When you hear the label medical doctor, hard-hat construction worker, investment banker, interior decorator, or big-data engineer, a mental image with long list of adjectives pops into your mind. Every culture invests each of its trades with a stereotype and a measure of prestige. You may even have chosen your line of work for precisely those accompanying attributes. You would not be the first physician who selected his field less for a love of healing than for the respect and a yacht dubbed *All Those Long Years in Medical School*. If such truly are your goals and this avenue satisfies them and you, then so be it. Just remember, your career title will doubtless define you in other's eyes, but it need not in yours.

Along with stereotypes, a more subtle career-defining belief may prove ruinous to your esteem and CEO self-mastery. It insists, "I am only what I have achieved." I am a book publisher. Well, how many books have you published today? This year? Even if I view myself within the richer career scope as a supplier of business-building information, I can still be haunted by the achievement exchequer demanding to audit my progress thus far. The moment you view yourself as just a banker or baker your career shrinks to a quantifiable nectar of numbers that you frantically labor to prop up.

When fate frowns from his seat as your board chair and your publishing, banking, or baking successes dwindle, these numbers will lure you into despair. After all, my rate of accomplishment in this field is the sole measure of my worth, right? Of course not. You know better. Not only is this itemized achievement ledger demeaning, as CEO you realize it is completely false. When you call in the business evaluators to appraise your company, do you want these folks to merely tally up the price and number of your products and deem that the total worth? That's but a minor part of the corporate value. Client contacts, good will, potential investment and revenues, possible earnings from inventive employees... the list of profitable assets current and future streams on and on. And do you think Your Marvelous Self should be hemmed by any lesser appraisal?

Shortly after authoring *The Art of the CEO*, I chatted with the leader of a large pharmaceutical firm. We met occasionally, and he had read my book without comment. Then one day he revealed to me that one sentence I'd tossed off at a gathering – a quip, in my mind a mere witticism – had totally changed his style of management and relations with all his corporate coworkers. From this far corner he'd found a great deal of help. It is impossible to measure the eventual effects of your entire self. So instead of counting your steps, why not keep on dancing under the choreography of your adventurous self as CEO?

The Art of Selection

The tap comes on your shoulder: what kind of trade do I want to wrap what kind of career around? What's the right job for my chosen trade? For how long? Do I even want to play this career game at all?

For you as Self CEO, few choices will ripple as widely as the career goals you shape and the trades you use to fill them. Your career will probably unlock your greatest abilities, call out your most dedicated efforts, and involve countless, devoted hours. The right career can take you to new zeniths of personal achievement. You may sip that heady exhilaration that comes from striving to your utmost – called arête by the ancient Greeks. And while it's not your sole weapon in the quest for the enriched life, 'tis one that you will draw often from your scabbard. Thus it pays to be careful, but not petrified.

Most folks fall into their first jobs and choose their trade almost as randomly. We blend abilities with opportunity and take a stab. No sin lies in this experimentation. After all, you've only someone else's estimation of whether this particular position will be a fit for you. According to the Bureau of Labor Statistics, throughout the past 35 years, the length of time American workers have held their current job has varied only slightly – between 3.7 and 4.2 years. More than three-quarters of US workers will change jobs within less than five years. Through all the economic roller coasters, we remain a nation of job hunters – our senses always alert for that next position that suits today's improved abilities and compensates more desirably.

If any flaw lies in this hope-driven trade hopping, it comes from neglecting to make the absolute most of your current situation before comparing it with those glimmering on the distant horizon. Answer the first needs first: does my current trade feed, clothe, and shelter me and my dependents? If it affords these basics, then don your CEO's cape and examine the current career and life potential.

Earlier, we defined career as a goal to be pursued with progressive expertise and achievement. The trade becomes a training session, driving you closer to your career goal and the contribution it makes. Is today's trade the sole best possible course for permanently guiding you toward that goal? Probably not. Well then, should you uproot and chase after the perfect trade or more career-enhancing job? That's a chief executive decision to be made with an eye on the benefits and cost of the change. To consider this leap, answer this checklist:

- Am I generally happy throughout the course of my workday?
- Do I feel fulfilled with what I am doing?
- Do I feel proud of my creation and contribution?
- Can I honestly say I hold a complete knowledge of my company and my trade? Have I explored every feature, connected job, and possible opportunity this current revenue source has to offer? Or am I judging my trade from my cubicle?
- Am I gaining expertise and progressing toward my stated career goal?
- Does this work fit with my principles and character?
- How important to me are the compensations of this current trade (e.g. remuneration, personal associations, prestige, and location)?
- How much job jumping can I – or my resume – afford, even if it's within my chosen trade?
- Answer quickly: what are the immediate and future opportunities available within my current job? (If it takes you more than five seconds to begin your answer, either get exploring or get out.)
- Wait a minute! Is this career goal I made during last semester of my senior year still current or obsolete? Have my sights shifted?

The Best Laid Plans....

Bill Endicott was the coach who led a group of young men and women amateur paddling athletes to America's first-ever world's championship in the esoteric, dangerous sport of whitewater canoe slalom. Bill welded these Washington, DC-area youngsters into a dedicated team. Under his guidance, they trained exhaustively, invented new stroke techniques, even designed and built their own boats. His athletes swept the sport. Bill's book, *To Win the Worlds*, sets out a much-emulated program of making one's "chosen goal the major emotional commitment" with all the devotion and sacrifice this demands.

It all seems very focused, and Bill Endicott sounds like the laser goaled individual who takes high aim and refuses to deviate. In truth, Bill Endicott set off for the nation's capital with no such intention. About a month before he left, Bill laid out his life's plan before me as we were making a canoe in a friend's garage. Bill was going to be a US senator. He had sent resumes and phoned several senators, and three of them had promised positions as aides. Step by step Bill explained the moves he would engineer to bring himself to that esteemed pinnacle of government service. Extremely intelligent and carefully educated, Bill Endicott had what it took. His mere telling of his plan excited me. Yet, as much as any man, Bill was the chief executive officer of his own life. He held the loftier aim of the richest possible life as his ultimate beacon. So when it came time to make that major emotional commitment, Bill Endicott selected the most fruitful of avenues.

One of the most admirable parts of Bill's career decision was that he was able to trim away all the irrelevant features of his career choice and remain steadfastly in pursuit to his life goals. His irrelevancies, of course, may not be yours.

Tips & Tasks Separate your self from your career vehicle. Almost invariably, your career will lead you into an alliance with some organization. Be it an enterprise you've launched or a group you've joined, your personal achievement will be linked with the growth and success of that organization. Linked – but not synonymous. The progress of your allied organization is not the true measure of you. As mentioned earlier, those countless interests, abilities, and desires that comprise the marvelous you flow far too broadly to be confined to a single program or goal.

The fact that his Edison Studios survived barely 30 less-than-stellar years in no way diminishes the immense contributions that Thomas Edison made in bringing reality-in-motion to the public domain. Thomas' two percent inspiration followed by his 98 percent perspiration completely changed how we view our world. Every cinematic competitor and successive filmmaker readily admits the great debt they owe Mr. Edison's genius and efforts. The career of Thomas Edison as film's founder soared gloriously, even though his faltering company rapidly passed the torch to others.

CEO of Yourself

Naturally you will develop a deeply personal attachment to those people and the whole corporate body that are helping you gallop forward. You are all striving together. Just remember, whatever allegiance you feel for your company cannot satisfyingly transcend your allegiance to yourself.

And what if you view this whole career game as unnecessary and not worth the effort? "Where's it written," you may well ask, "that I have to be in progressive pursuit of anything?" 'Tis a worthy consideration to be honestly addressed.

Why Work?

Your priest insists, "You owe it to society to take a contributing job." Your psychiatrist suggests, "You owe it to yourself." But the anthropologist, I believe, holds a more instructive answer: "You work because you simply cannot help yourself." Each of us has a creative itch to scratch. We all feel surges of joy whenever we're sweating and building something. It's in our blood.

Compared to most other animals, we *Homo sapiens* are poorly planned for both offense and defense. As prey, we are slow, visible, thin-skinned, unarmored, and very chewy. As predators, we lack the highly developed weaponry of the great blue heron, T-rex, or retractably clawed felines. Our sole survival advantage lies in our frenzied urge to make stuff. We are always making new weapons, defenses, coverings, and castles. Anthropologists note with wonder the human phenomenon termed "island madness." Even when a human culture does find a haven where food and shelter come easily, we gobble up our leisure hours erecting massive pyramids or Easter Island statues. Idle hands somehow annoy us. You're simply not fulfilled unless you can grab some tools, shift your huge brain into high gear, and make your days flourish.

Your labors, as with your own forged principles, must be undertaken for your own benefit. If they bring no benefit to you, they cannot efficiently carry you toward a fulfilling life. For this reason, this author, like Theodore Roosevelt, preaches the "gospel not of ignoble ease, but of the strenuous life." I have yet to meet the individual who has found complete joy and life enrichment through a course of mental, physical, and spiritual inactivity. However, that is simply one man's experience. Your chosen course may just prove me dead wrong. **BB**

Afterthought ♋

In 1912, accomplished musician and theologian Albert Schweitzer landed in Gabon (then French Equatorial Africa), not as an evangelical preacher, but with the career goal of bettering the human condition of the Lambarene Mission District. To progress this career pursuit, Rev. Schweitzer had taken a medical degree. He founded a hospital and church, then financed both by his organ concerts and writings. All his abilities came into play, including his astounding make-more-with-less money-managing skill. In the end, Schweitzer accomplished his career goal of improving conditions for the people of the Lambarene Mission District. And he was awarded the Nobel Peace Prize for his philosophy of Reverence of Life. The broader one's career contribution, the more trades are required and richer one's journey through life becomes.

CEO of Yourself

Chapter 10

Got Ambition?

Ambition is a dream with a V8 engine.

– Elvis Presley

It positively drips with connotation. Ambition. Few words in the English language can so launch, prod, provoke, annoy, and inspire otherwise happily complacent individuals. Yet for most folks, the comprehension of ambition's massive artillery ends at the tip of its trigger.

So what is it? Ambition is that yearning for some hopefully fulfillable goal. We all have it to varying degrees. It is an emotion we unleash from our deepest essence to gain whatever we believe we need for satisfaction. Ambition forever seeks, if you will, the orgasm of achievement. How much ambition we bank behind a certain project or career depends on our personal desires and the value we place on the compensation offered. Ambition fixes our eyes unwaveringly on the goal. The prize is the prime concern.

For example, it demands very little ambition for this author to pen the pages of this book because I really enjoy writing it. My drive to accomplish this book and imbue each sentence with optimum meaning is fed by my personal delight in the writing. At the same time, I hold an immense ambition within my life to achieve the book's perceived compensations (cash, fame, and providing vital wisdom). The lure of these goals accompanies my love of the process. I lean on both to spark my enthusiasm. It's just that for this particular project, I lean mostly on the latter. However, if my publisher were foolish enough to have me compose a computer manual, I would have to summon every ounce of my ambitious fervor to grind out the first chapter.

The Key

Whatever level of ambition you hold for your career, life, or any project – that is the correct amount. Ambition is one of the most honestly felt emotions. You want what you want, but on your every craving you set individual limits. Your boss may dress up the goals to coax a higher level of ambition out of you. Parents and teachers may scold you and try forcefully to convince you that you should want what you want more passionately, but it's a sham. You cannot fake desire. And why would you? Of course, you can put on a courtship display of clench-jawed ambition. (Remember that seething zeal you showed during your last job interview?) But that's mere playacting to make an impression. At the end of the day, your passion for life or any of its parts will evolve naturally as an honest reflection of your circumstances. As Self CEO, respect your ambition level and don't let anyone bully you into faux feelings. And for heaven's sake, don't ever feel guilty or bully yourself.

Like any emotion, ambition is dynamic and evolves with the flow of events. For over 25 years Dr. Ann Hanrahan was an energetically devoted histologist, studying the tissues of one minor group of small slugs. She loved her work and radiated a strong ambition to see her research through to its conclusion. Then came the discovery: one enzyme from one animal seemed very probably to hold a life-saving treatment for AIDS victims. Ann's already fervent ambition ratcheted up to near frenzy. She practically lived in her lab. The compensations for her research had mushroomed exponentially. Her ambition rose with the new conditions.

Ann's boost in ambition came with unusual suddenness. More typically, ambition – unlike anger, lust, and fear – is an emotion that eases in subtly on a tide of interest. Gradually, as we labor along at some enterprise, a new perspective seeps in, revealing more valuable compensations. Our desire to accomplish swells and enthusiasm takes seed.

Blunders to Avoid Humans cannot thrive on ambition alone. Undertaking a way of life or career you daily loathe, all for the hopes of grand rewards in the sweet bye-and-bye, is a guaranteed recipe for misery. Eventually, as success begins to wane, the brittle chain of ambitious compensation will snap, and all that endured sacrifice and resentment will burst forth, flooding you with depression. When framing your life and work, why not piece together a satisfying blend of enjoyable daily process and fulfilling goals?

The Exceptional Thirst

Chris Blees is kind, warm, generous, and endearingly friendly. He is also among the top 10 legally most ambitious folks you'll ever encounter. Chris is one of those exceptional individuals who holds a magma-hot passion for life in general and for every goal he seeks to achieve. Starting as an accountant for BiggsKofford CPA firm in Colorado Springs, Chris has rapidly risen to CEO. Upon realizing that so many of his skills might garner infinitely greater rewards in the investment banking arena, Chris became an investment banker. He launched and headed a banking division for BiggsKofford Capital, designing it to handle the full range of mergers and acquisitions. By offering banking, investment counseling, and accounting services, BiggsKofford now claims clients worldwide. Shortly after joining the Alliance of Merger & Acquisition Advisors professional organization, Chris introduced innovative concepts that led to his being elected leader of the AMAA's course-creation team. He is currently a renowned dealmaker and sought-after lecturer in his field.

In his down time, Chris is a competitive marathoner and triathlete, training with his wife on long bike rides through the Rockies. Also an expert mountaineer, Chris is joined on the trail by his adventurous son, with whom he routinely undertakes expeditions to higher summits. For this man, seeking out new goals and striving to achieve them has become a calling. Challenge is a habit.

From where does it spring? Those sparkling persons who are always questing higher hurdles, always reaching a little further for a second helping of life's feast – what's stoking their fire, and how can I get me some? In short, if any one trait of character distinguishes those who glow with ambition's fire, it is the unshakable belief in two things:

- **Their course** They truly believe that if they hurl their utmost efforts along their chosen path, it will undoubtedly lead them to accomplishing their goals.
- **Their goals** They truly believe that achieving each chosen goal will bring ultimate satisfaction and fulfillment.

The greater your faith in these two beliefs, the greater will grow your passionate ambition to bring them about.

Obviously, such faith, however certain, may crumble under the pummeling of reality. Raging ambition requires a fair and steady flow of success.

A really ambitious devotee may be able to convince herself of both these beliefs. Yes, if I can just land the entry-level roles, my acting career will soar to stardom and it will shower me with happiness and fulfillment. That success is all I require. But such faith may not bear up under the crush of a few hundred of fruitless auditions. You may plunge along your course with a nearly delusional self-confidence in your capability to seize the goal, and you may just as thoroughly fail. Fail often enough, and ambition will abandon you. Keep on persisting with no glimmer of hopeful success, and you may, like one capable man I knew, scribble across your business plan, "The dream is dead. Just do the work."

Tips & Tasks 'Tis a sad but important truth: neither wishing nor wanting makes it so. Increasing the intensity of your personal ambition will not affect your likelihood of obtaining either success or fulfillment. Further, there is no guaranteed correlation between unstinting hard labor and success. Victory seldom sits on the shoulders of the most deserving. As CEO in charge of effectively executing your choices, periodically bring your prime path and goals under review. Honestly assess:

▶ Will this set of compensations I'm aiming at still bring me personal fulfillment?

▶ And if so, is there a more efficient course to land them in my lap?
   In the words of Chris Blees, "Planning works better than salesmanship."

Too Much of a Good Thing?

The whole world loves ambition. We prize it in ourselves, and we use it as a final judgment on others. Interestingly, we tend to measure ambition by how much an individual is willing to sacrifice to grasp his chosen goal. 'Tis not an entirely inaccurate yardstick. Make the reward important enough to me personally, and I will yield up my cash, my cherished weekends with loved ones, my self-respect, perhaps even my morality and health to gain what I perceive is vital. Society heaps laurels on such sacrificers and insists that more ambition you've got, the better.

But think for a moment. Take a look at the Ambition Ladder. The majority of folks clamber somewhere around the low middle. This 85 percent of working stiffs have each developed some particular expertise that they daily perform. Sure, they'd like a raise or promotion, and they are willing to put on a one-time work spurt to gain it, but for the most part they seek neither challenges nor great changes. They are the resignedly content. And that's not really tragic because they are granted a fair wage, and they gain the additional compensation of feeling justifiably good about themselves and their achievements on their journey home.

Grasping at the higher rungs come the strivers. Abraham Lincoln fit into this category. "Abe is like a ticking watch," noted his law partner William Herndon. "You can always hear his mind ticking on how he can turn this particular situation to his best advantage." Maybe one rung nearby clambers business magnate Warren Buffett. Early in his career, upon reading a newspaper piece about a broker with a revolutionary investing strategy, young Buffett leapt from his chair, boarded a train, then, after a several-hundred-mile rail trip, raced to this investor's office and began pounding on his door. The men met and it seems to have worked well for Warren. He still ravenously pushes onward in search of the next, best investment. Achievers at this high level retain our admiration.

But they are not the highest summiters on ambition's ladder. The utmost rungs belong to those driven to risk beyond reason. They are propelled by some single salvation at the expense of all else. At this wobbly pinnacle scrabble ruthless gangsters, like Alphonse Capone's "enforcer," Frank Nitti, who launched his business career by killing a man for a wheelbarrow load of vegetables. Climbing vigorously alongside him are Russian mob head Semion Mogilevich, who rose to power as a contract killer, and Japan's Kenichi Shinoda, whose personal ambitions infect society with extortion, violence, human trafficking, and countless miseries.

These persons willingly set aside their most basic humanity. They slaughter unconcernedly and ignore the misfortune they spread. Their insatiable craving to achieve their aims, far exceeding Lincoln's or Buffett's, brings the entire wrath of society down on themselves. No deed, nor any sacrifice lies out of bounds in meeting their ambitions. Such are the people who roost at the very top of ambition's ladder.

Those who unbridle their ambition and set it galloping unheeded across life's field will also sacrifice self-mastery. They cease to be a CEO who thoughtfully assesses vision, goals, and outcomes. They are driven – not driving. They become victims of a single, all-encompassing urge, winning neither admiration nor fulfillment.

Got Ambition?

The Ambition Handle

"We want ambitious people to work for us," reads the sign on the glass door of a local restaurant chain. You bet they do. Every human resource interviewer and company owner sings endless hymns of praise to ambition because it makes the employee possessing it a very useable tool. Displaying that strong desire to rise and achieve sprouts a handle from your back with a large sign announcing, "Steer Me. I'm Easy." The more you ambitiously seek some enterprise's promised reward, the simpler it is to get you to work overtime, follow corporate rules, forsake office romance, and sacrifice for the owner who dangles that salvation before you.

This is not altogether a bad thing. Worthy goals do indeed demand sacrifice. What you give up in your trade for what you expect to receive is a standard part of your negotiations. Most jaw-droppingly-salaried financial brokers began paying their dues with mind-numbing months in the cold-calling pit, dialing for new investor dollars all the day long. Darn few love this process, but they lean heavily on their ambitions to get this sacrificial part of the job done. So must we all, at times.

How much rein you give your ambitions is one of your chief executive decisions. And it is one that must be frequently reevaluated. You understand fully that work and life supervisors will try to seize the handle and play on your ambitions. They are not your enemy. As manager or leader, you will probably do the same. They are simply persuaders presenting you with an honest choice. You are the CEO best equipped to make this choice because no one more than you has your own interests at heart. Ambition's choices are truly yours.

Oh, one final note about displaying eagerness to gobble up life and career goals: there is nothing more ugly than naked ambition. No one wants to behold your private, greedy needs exposed. So it is best to cloak it in a love of hard work. Friends, colleagues, even supervisors would much prefer to set their eyes on a worker who revels in pushing the project forward than witnessing some frantic soul desperately sacrificing for an eventual goal. Let them gaze upon your best side. BB

Afterthought ❧

More mornings than not, young Joseph would go down to the river that flowed through his small Hungarian village and dig his fingers into the rich bankside mud. Kneeding this soft earth, he would bring forth figures of his own imaginings. Back home, he watched his father, a cobbler, reshape and design all his tools so they fit his hands perfectly – a technique the boy took to heart. In school, Joseph took every opportunity to sculpt in all materials. He was encouraged and studied avidly under the best artists available. Joseph's abilities and his impressive productivity were noted.

Not long after completing his education, Joseph Petrovics earned great renown with several major commissions and, at a markedly early age, was appointed premier sculptor in Hungary. Later, after emigrating to the United States, he received a string of enviable commissions and began training the most talented students in his adopted nation. Today, New York City visitors to Ground Zero stand awed before Joseph Petrovics' 56-foot bronze mural immortalizing the firefighters who fought so valiantly to save lives as the Twin Towers came crashing down on September 11, 2001. Currently, more days than not, Joseph may be found at his Blawenberg NJ studio. When he is not working on commissions, he devotes his restless energy to arranging stone walls and towers around his property. He is still following his boyhood proclivity. The most serene folks seem to be those who receive a little encouragement to do what they already love to do.

CEO of Yourself

Chapter 11

Cultivating Your Staff

One iron-willed, ambitious individual can climb the highest mountain, but one compassionate person working with all his supporters can move it. –BJ

More people want to help you than hurt you.

One thing that separates this guide from the mountain of scribbled pages urging you toward self-mastery is that this one opens the door and shoves you outside in your quest for fulfillment. There's no restricting you to the small cabinet of your inner core where you rummage for some ever-stiffening resolve. Instead, we coax you to explore, lift your eyes, see new choices, and mingle Your Marvelous Self with others. You live in a swiftly flowing, very real, crowded, and very exciting world. The enrichment you seek lies in the most unexpected corners. And while going it alone with rugged individualism offers a certain smug pride, it is just plain inefficient. Even Julius Caesar stopped to ask directions when conquering Gaul.

The victors in this life grab eagerly at every advantage. Their accomplishments are not diminished by enlisting aid or advice; rather, their goals mushroom with the number of supporters they win to their side. So it is with your enterprise. The corporation of you is about to take wing. Comrades, advisors, and a wealth of incidental acquaintances stand waiting to sweeten your days and help you grow toward your goals. 'Tis time to assemble your team.

Who's on Board?

The question of who is on your staff is reminiscent of the lawyer who asked Jesus Christ, "Who is my neighbor?" In one sense, everyone is. Each person whose words you read, encounter on your morning commute, every guest at that seemingly boring party, even your wretched enemy may provide you with some wise nugget, sparkling experience, or a bitter yet worthwhile lesson.

As Self CEO, think of these peripheral folks as your outsourced contractors, your suppliers – your second-tier support team. They are acquaintances who, mostly inadvertently, contribute to the richness of your life. Even though you may scarcely know them, they are vital. You'd be lost without the constant influx of their stimulating assistance. It falls to you to cultivate this army of aid. You must put yourself in the way of these suppliers and keep their riches streaming in. Work to develop Your Marvelous Self as an inviting and rewarding oasis for the wealth of experiences and knowledge they have to offer.

Closer and more frequently met are the people in your first-tier support team: coworkers, cronies, confidantes, all types of mentors, friends, family, and your mental board of directors. They form your in-factory staff. This being real life, first-tier affiliates seldom fall into a single category. Roger may serve as a mental board member who reminds you of your chosen principles, as an expert who enhances your art appreciation, and as an intimate, nonjudgmental confidante. Odds are excellent that even Roger remains unaware of all his support roles. But you must be.

The chief executive officer draws each of these people to himself in harmonious collaboration. 'Tis all part of a joyous process of sharing and feeding each others' mutual energies. Together they form an ever-growing personal network – individual allies maintained by your constant care.

The unique element of the Self CEO's team is that the members are seldom united. They are more of a staff, each contracted singly, each lending his/her efforts, joined primarily by their concern for you. Your husband may only vaguely know your workplace mentor. Your dearest, most confidential friend may provide guidance in dealing with coworkers and other acquaintances he has never met. And there is typically no real advantage in pushing them together. Avoid the temptation to team build. Your spouse does not really need to meet your imam or rock-climbing instructor. Unless – and this is a big unless– you can envision some shared benefit in their meeting. As servant leader, you are ever on the lookout to advance every person in tier 1 (those close individuals you know) and tier 2 (casual encounters). You stand at the center of your web; you alone know everyone in this network. And just as you are driven to grasp the resources they hold, you seek to enrich their lives. So upon learning that your neighbor and boss share a passion for chess, you, as a CEO, physically bring them together. You take the time. It feeds them, it feeds your heart, and it is the best investment you will ever make.

Tier 1 – Recruiting Top Talent

The greatest recruitment tool for bringing folks eagerly to your side is your own distinctive passion. See your neighbor John casually picking up small branches off his lawn and you'll probably pass by disinterestedly. But spy that same neighbor sweating with all his might and muscle to heft a huge stone into his rock garden, and you will naturally be moved to lend a hand. His passion is instinctively contagious. You cannot help it. The intensity of John's desire sparks yours. We humans are magnetized by excitement. Any time we see one of our fellows energetically laboring toward some directed goal, we want to join in and give a push.

That is the essence of leadership. The deeper your craving to achieve and the more visibly you display that craving, the more your first-tier associates will be motivated to contribute support. Then, to ice the cake, if the leader can effectively convince his team that his achievement will reward them, their motivation and commitment are sure to follow.

Since you know and regularly meet most of your first-tier staff members, you may already be sharing a few mutual interests. You may pass around their expertise to others. Thus the challenge becomes to let these people witness your goals and conjure an appropriate reward. In the case of neighbor John, his thanks and compliment on your muscle power might be enough. Or he might even brag to another passing neighbor about your prowess. Simple, thoughtful, and effective. Recruiting others to your side forces you to develop and display the noble art of appreciation.

As CEO of Your Marvelous Self, you have taken aim at the richer, more fulfilling life that you know lies out there for you. To achieve this vision, you probably have broken it down into specific goals: respect at work, high adventures in faraway places, a flourishing vineyard, friendship, and romantic love. Aiming at these goals, you realize that you need to expand your first-tier staff and bring aboard comrades possessing certain lines of expertise. You require the guidance of a vintner, matchmaker, business mentor, or mountaineering partner.

At this point, the mediocre CEO would assess his goals, determine the skills required to reach them, and begin rounding up a staff of people, each possessing some narrow expertise. Sounds very direct and logical. But you are not a mediocre chief executive officer. You are not about to hunt for little pieces of people to cram into rigid goal slots. Forget focusing on skillsets. Seek and cultivate the acquaintance of whole, interesting persons, filled with, among other talents, the ability to warmly and wisely feed your experience.

Somehow, in this process of developing new staff members, looms the temptation to build hierarchies of support. We ruinously begin placing ourselves and our friends on some artificial scale of worth and obligation. He's worth more to me than I am to him. We begin piling up ledgers of debt vs. value given, forgetting that we all are just fellow travelers, helping each other along. Take a look at the following story. Have you ever played any of these roles?

Levelling the Field

At age nine, Bill looks around the playground, spies Cathy, and asks, "Hey Cath, wanna kick the soccer ball around?" No qualms, no anxieties. He's just asking. No big deal. Fast forward five years. Bill approaches Cathy again, this time trying to get a date for the middle school dance. "Um, ah, Cathy....I was wondering...if, ah...." With head down, Bill bumbles out his invitation, wishing he could have just texted her. The difference? The equality has vanished. Nudged along by social norms and some very mysterious urges, Bill now sees himself as a beggar seeking a boon from a pedestaled being. He has mentally set himself on a one-way street in which he eagerly wants, but cannot imagine anything he has to give. Bill's painful awkwardness derives from his mentally placing Cathy on that higher pedestal. She didn't climb up; he set her there.

Fast forward another 15 years. Cathy, having risen to the rank of Acme Widget's chief innovation officer, is desperately seeking a new product line. Bill, a mere rank and file mechanic at Acme, boasts no track record whatsoever but possesses an encyclopedic knowledge of the widget market. He holds the answer to Cathy's prayers. But Cathy ignores Bill's exhaustive plans dropped into the company suggestion box because she has placed Bill in a ditch beneath her. She's destroyed the equality and with it her opportunity to gain and accept his aid.

As a happy ending to this allegory, we move forward another four years when Bill and Cathy meet at their high school reunion. Bill gives Cathy a wink and slyly says, "Hey Cath, wanna kick the soccer ball around?" And within minutes, they abandon the party and are running around the soccer field in their party rags, hooting and laughing with a whole lot of mutually shared fun. No qualms, no big deal. Just asking.

If, as the great religions teach, we are all equal in the eyes of the Lord, why not view others through these divine lenses?

Recruiting Tier 2

The whole concept of enlisting aid from an army of strangers strikes many folks as a distasteful broccoli moment. All the lure of delightful chance encounters, enlightening conversations, valued advice, and fresh companions is quickly soured by the wincing challenge of throwing themselves into an unfamiliar and probably unlovable crowd. A great percentage of us are reticent when approaching others for any reason, and for support most of all. Some folks are merely solitary by nature. Others call themselves "shy," which is code for being scared of others – both known and unknown.

The challenge may be daunting, but as chief executive officer you cannot afford to ignore resources. You know that a better life lies out there, and these temporary strangers are the assets that can deliver pieces of it. 'Tis foolish to let these opportunities slip by. In all my years in business, I have never heard one successful CEO say, "It is such a bother to talk with new clients. We have enough now, so let's not trouble ourselves getting any more."

Attitude Adjustment You possess the wealth of self to offer what others really desire. So do they. This makes all human contact a sharing. You meet and swap selves, thoughts, stories. If you can see each chance encounter as this innocent and harmless you can shed the baggage of obligation, comparative rank, and second-guessing the judgment of others. Work to strip your mind of all these presumptions, and the fearful wall separating you from others will tumble down. Remember, lead with your curiosity, not your need. You are sharing first and seeking only tangentially.

Engage! W.S. Gilbert, in his 1887 poem "Etiquette," spins a tale about two upper-crust Englishmen who lived together on a desert island for years, never speaking because they had not been properly introduced. Fortunately, we have moved into an age when the value of spreading one's circle of acquaintances is deemed greater than protocol. Under today's norm, all of us are now learning to style ourselves as open and approachable.

You have doubtless worked out your own rules of engagement and are developing them as you go. A few additional tactics that may prove successful include:

▶ Prepare to greet the world armed with a few quotes, funny one-liners, and interesting facts. This way, when you announce out loud, seemingly to no one in particular, "You know, twenty years ago, this city had half the people and only one third the cars it's got now," you've provided the stranger an opportunity to bite or leave your bait alone.
▶ Sample several organizations. Put yourself into good company. Attend gatherings of local clubs and activity groups. Try a walk with an outing club or drop in on the professional group to which your boss belongs. Join a charity board, the county historical society, your church's food distribution center, or the chapter of the Lions, Elks, and Order of Moose. (Networking parties don't count.) When you find a fit, offer your services.
▶ Carry and be ready to proffer personal cards. Our favorite: "Richard Rowe, Dragon Slayer" (phone and e-mail included). Cards are rectangles of hope that, after reveling in the meeting of the moment, your delight may be continued.
▶ Make social media more social than media. Instead of posting a self-laudatory photo with some bent-to-impress comment, why not post the pix of your new-found acquaintance and caption it with one of this person's specific achievements or bits of expertise?
▶ Get comfortable. You don't have to prowl for enriching souls every waking moment. Follow your mood.

CEO of Yourself

On two separate occasions, the same friend asked me, "You have so many friends, how do you find them all?" and "Why do you surround yourself with so many losers?" Coupling these two queries makes the answers obvious. Every creature on this terrestrial orb holds some gift. It is the CEO's job to assess, select, and enlist every advantage by sifting through as many as possible. The more active his search, the richer his corporate self grows. A further CEO task is keeping the important interludes alive. The most common and disastrous crime of leaders is to let relationships die of neglect. Follow up on the best leads.

Tips & Tasks Remember to always celebrate your success with those contributing to it. The famous Oktoberfest that explodes across Germany every autumn began as a giant and festive thank-you party. Back when farm work was all sweat, performed by many hands, every farmer counted on his neighbors to pitch in with the immense and frantic labor of bringing in the harvest. The celebratory gathering afterward was each family's way of paying back the others who had contributed to meet their neighbors' needs.

What makes Oktoberfest such fun is that no tally is kept; no one emphasizes the obligation. It all centers around the food and warm sense of community. For our family, it's our annual pig roast that we throw for about a hundred or so close friends whom we thank for the innumerable ways they have enriched our year. Our many staff members (comrades) behold our great joy and good fortune, and each guest realizes his/her part in it – amidst beer, bagpipes, songs, and fine feasting. ▆▆

Afterthought

Thomas Edward Lawrence, best remembered as Lawrence of Arabia, acted as an army of one during the First World War, performing some of the most amazing feats of leadership ever recorded. Under a series of comingled titles from the British military based in Egypt, Lawrence set forth to consolidate the Arab tribes around the Mediterranean in revolt against the Ottoman Turks who ruled the region. Lawrence's abilities to incorporate the internally warring factions of the Arab peoples and promote their independence with European imperialist powers were masterful to the point of mysterious. Yet one Lawrence leadership element stands out as particularly effective.

As the Arab troops prepared to lay siege to Aqaba and later Damascus, Lawrence's snow white thobe (robe) and keffiyeh (head covering) appeared everywhere within sights of the Turkish guns. Seemingly oblivious to the danger, Lawrence moved calmly among the positions, encouraging the troops, laying in equipment, standing openly on hilltops while giving orders. His terrifying intensity of will and fervor inspired others to protect him. British General Allenby wistfully notes that Lawrence was defended by "men of wild and most adventurous sprit...among those wild and reckless rangers there was not one who would not have willingly died for their chief." The ranks of these bodyguards were the most competitive in all the Arabian regiments. The force of steely determination will magnetize a devoted team to the side of an admirable leader.

CEO of Yourself

Chapter 12

Sustaining Your Corporation

It is more important for Enthusiasm to rest on your shoulder than Victory. _ BJ

In ancient Greece, Athena, goddess of wisdom, was often shown with a homely owl resting quietly on her shoulder. This totem was Victory, known to the Greeks as Nike. No, this owl did not wear running shoes, nor did she carry messages to Hogworts students. She did, however, symbolize the fleeting and fickle nature of victory, flitting whimsically through this unfair life. We all want victory to settle on us. But there is more to life than triumph.

Look at your goals. Bicycling across lower Tibet will not permanently build you an enriched life. Pile onto that achievement: respect and rewards at work, your art study tour of Europe's grandest cathedrals, and building the home you always wanted. You're still not there. Even romantic love full feasted is something short of utter fulfillment. All of these adventures ignite sparks, but they themselves are not the full fire of the life you set out to seize. That enriched life glows with a burning ember of enthusiasm that rages to a blaze with each new adventure. You discover yourself waking eager to tackle today's prospects. You like where you are, and you want more sunrises. You may feel that fire surge when you've finally gained that promotion, remained sober for three days, even when you disappointedly limp across the 10K finish line at the back of the pack.

You have fallen in love with the trying, the doing, the experience. Success may briefly feed your fire, but failure cannot dampen it. Those defining CEO adjectives discussed earlier – eager, principled, active, inquisitive, fearless, involved, and stubborn – seem more and more to describe how you feel and see yourself. You are doing more of what you want, and whatever the results, it is you who have directed them. You're the rain-maker, and that's darn satisfying. Nike may not be nailed to your shoulder, but these days, life truly tastes a lot sweeter.

Using the tools of vision, character, and principles, you have built the product: a person you like. The Corporation of You Unlimited is up, running, and paying strong dividends. Wonderful. You always knew Your Marvelous Self could do it. Grab some time to celebrate and fondly review your accomplishments. Just remember that the life you seek is not a prize, but a process. You are a dynamic being. Desires change and grow with experience. Those absolutely must-have cravings you had at age 13 are not those you hold today. And now that you have raised your vision, new goals and yearnings flood in all the faster.

As chief executive officer, you have to constantly update that original prototypical life path. Corporate business calls it product innovation. A growing company must bring in new, beneficial enhancements that make the entire product experience richer and more attractive to the customer. We are not suggesting change for change's sake. Rather, as CEO, you will keep tabs on your evolving self and find new tactics that sustain the excitement in the odyssey you are proposing.

Gifts to Yourself

To prevent each day from lapsing into stale repetition and to keep enthusiasm's fire firmly glowing as you travel (or dance) along life's course, you'd better look alive. Enthusiasm and her brother Ambition are elusive. Like coy lovers, they must be courted by a series of continuous gifts. We suggest these six:

Sartre Moments* ∾ Since you are your own CEO and customer, your fulfillment journey tends to roll along without much feedback. No company executive rings you up, asking how you, as client, are enjoying your route this far. Thus, set time apart and cultivate profitable self-to-self talk. Arrange those precious periods of thoughtful solitude when you monitor the shape and direction of your being. Donning an attitude of total honesty, assess your joy. Do your selected principles still apply? What do you think of your character? Then ponder through those recent goals.

Footnote: *Existential philosopher Jean-Paul Sartre, who brought to light the radical freedom we humans possess, was an adamant advocate of the benefits of productive solitude. We use the term Sartre Moments in homage to this great thinker.*

CEO of Yourself

As an insightful CEO, hold these new desires up to scrutiny to determine if they are truly yours or some invasive plant from a begging solicitor maneuvering to win you to her regime.

With this client input in mind, summon your bravery and begin adjusting that life journey with an eye toward the future – even if the present seems fine just now.

Diverse Adventures ⟋ You are not a solopreneur. Your Marvelous Self is a rich, multi-diverse corporation. Your satisfaction extends far beyond the bounds of your career or garden. Throughout these pages we have encouraged you to explore – to keep your antennae up, engage new people, and plunge into novel experiences. Hopefully, that why-not? spirit will mingle with your can-do executiveship and pump curiosity through your veins. Even when desire is lacking, call upon a broccoli moment of discipline and experiment with some new undertaking. As venturesome Eleanor Roosevelt was fond of suggesting, "Do something that scares you every day."

It may be a single, grand expedition, like that of dedicated spinal surgeon Mike, who sabbaticalized his spirit, stepped from the stern bonds of his medical career, and headed north to Alaska. Upon arriving, he served as an assistant to an Iditarod racer as she prepared for the rugged 1000-mile dog sled race. Mike accompanied her over what he termed the most God-awful and beautiful terrain on earth.

Or you may indulge in a more ritual release, as does pharmaceutical researcher Marie, who auditions for some small part and performs each month at her community's little theater. One of the finest gifts ever to land in my Christmas stocking came from my wife, who signed me up for a series of piano lessons. I have joyfully continued this new art these past three years, playing and practicing very much to my own delight, if perhaps less so for those within earshot. (Who's on your gift list?)

Each new individual encountered holds an adventure. Each community embodies dozens of various activity groups awaiting your experimental participation. We cannot urge you strongly enough to push aside the veil of fear and inertia and touch the untried. O taste and see.

The Gift of Health ❧ Right at this reading, you are nursing some injury, you are gaining strength, and you are dealing with some very beneficial and some very destructive health choices. Such is the state of all individuals on this terrestrial orb. One comparatively new element in our human scenario – barely a century old – is the increased ability for many individuals living within the protection of today's miraculous medicines to greatly govern their own health.

Yes, fate still sits in your board chair seat and can toss you leprosy or a sucking chest wound at any moment. And yes, we are all terminal. Yet, for most living in first-world cultures, life has become considerably less dangerous and less taxing. For these fortunate folks, choosing a well-designed and disciplined regimen of mental and physical exercises, attentive medical repairs, and a nutritionally based diet can add a great wealth to their lives.

Sculptor Joseph Petrovics claims it is that breakfast of two heaping handfuls of raw vegetables that sustains his energy and clears his vision as he enters his studio. For TriNet CEO Burton Goldfield, the confidence packed on from his weightlifting carries through into his demanding career. For retired Exxon toxicologist Rick McKee closing in on age 70, it's those daily 50-mile bike rides that keep him moving like a man half his age. And Thora Bonnell always insisted it was two-hours of morning piano practice, maintained from her youth, that sharpened mind and memory throughout her nearly five score years. Such investments truly bolster today's capabilities and better your odds for prolonging them through the years.

For the Self CEO, health choices are less clear than we are led to believe. Your body might thank you if you never experienced a glass of wine, never played a contact sport, and always avoided straining your physical self right up to the danger point. But would you be the better for it? Do the measured shackles of moderation hold the key to the enriched and happy life? Your call.

Blunders to Avoid We all tend to fall in love with certain practiced disciplines to the neglect of others. We know one very careful, diet-conscious vegan who is appallingly lax when stricken with a medical condition that demands long study of physicians and treatment options. How many friends do you have who scrupulously train either mind or body, while ignoring the other? As CEO, you hold the responsibility for tending the entire temple and improving to the utmost your every asset. For whatever discipline you adopt, habit will be your most effective aid in sustaining it. With continued repetition every act in life eases into habit. From bedtime teeth brushing to that little gesture indicating embarrassment, when performed over and over, it becomes a triggered response. Your decision process gets short-circuited, and you respond instinctively. Your eyes register, "Oh, red light," and the foot automatically hits the brake. Nothing will so help you wrestle with temptation as developing your healthy choices into habits. They're called Broccoli Moments because most of us are not desperately drawn to enact the choice we know is best for ourselves. But with time, those awakening exercises, that evening meditation, and bypassing the pastry tray will all lapse into ritual. Just one caveat: have you sorted through your personal list of habits and checked which need to be weeded out or resown – for your own sake?

Oh, and for the love of yourself, make choices that are enjoyable. Don't do fitness. Do fun.

Endurance ❧ It is one of the most effective values you can weld onto your character. And currently, alas, it is one of the most neglected. Yet still it calls to us from a previous era.

Back in the 19th century, when polar exploring ships were sagely christened *Endurance*, an individual's iron resolve took lofty rank among his most treasured values. School children learned Rudyard Kipling's character-forging poem *"If"* which urged them to "hold on when there is nothing in you except the will that says, 'Hold on.'" Folks were no more noble then. It was merely a time when inescapable burdens heaped upon people, and the only solution was to endure, hopefully with a grin.

Today, we don't endure – we innovate. We witness human engineering transforming our environs and medicine's astounding advances, and we mistakenly conclude that humanity is the absolute repairer of all ills. Then, when a crushing load of circumstance falls, most people collapse. They simply are not trained to endure anything that cannot be fixed. And endurance is entirely a matter of training.

No one is genetically predisposed to withstand pain, loss, hunger, or ceaseless failure. Very rapidly after our entrance into this world, we discover that life is not a bowl of cherries, and we learn to endure the denial of this wish and that one. We stop the ineffective whining; we shift our attention from our fantasy wish list and find satisfaction in realms of reality. As we grow, the pain and tribulations increase. The successful among us continue nurturing this seed of endurance.

And nothing nurtures endurance, desensitizes the hurt, and diminishes the fear like a little repetitive training. Forget the naked plunges into icy seas or acrophobia-battling free-climbs up electric towers, a la G. Gordon Liddy. Try a few physical activities, such as riding your bicycle standing for two minutes, without dropping onto the seat – then three minutes. Or perhaps fasting one day a week. How strong is your will? There are scores of such small exercises you can build into your day that will tap into your deep, unexpected well of resolve. Such brief tests bring this resolve to the surface. The required emotions of pride, ambition, joy, even pieces of anger and hate, will trigger frequently. Then when the real challenge strikes, they will come to the fore.

Training tip: Take pride in Your Marvelous Self. Celebrate your personal endure-ability. Distract your focus from the misery of your load and let your chest swell with the impressive size of what you are able to bear – with a grin.

One gentleman in my neighborhood, seeking to toughen his feet, takes delight in walking barefoot outside through all seasons. A neighbor, once spying his naked toes as he scuffed through freshly fallen snow asked, "Isn't that cold?"

To which Bart drew back a broad smile and replied, "Oh God, yes." And continued on his walk.

Keeping Up the Yuks ∾ When was the last time you got really giddy? When you and a group of conspiratorial cronies sat cracking wise with everyone laughing and each line feeling funnier than the last? 'Tis a contagion devoutly to be wished from time to time. Laughter is, among many other things, a sign of good health. "So if you can laugh at this joke," says the doctor, "I'll give you a clean bill."

Having humor in your soul is much more than a joke repertoire. It is a thoughtful and pleasurable perspective on your life situation. Humor forces you up a 300-foot ladder to gain an overview of what you are doing. So when you, as director of marketing, climb up that ladder, see

CEO of Yourself

this job for what it really is, you can clamber back down and announce to your team, "You know folks, marketing is the art of pinning pears on an apple tree and selling them as exotic." You all chuckle – and reflect a little thoughtfully about what you all are doing at this job anyway.

And when the joke does get told, a brief unity spreads through the group. One of your coworkers shakes his head and notes, "When our board of directors calls the roll, half these guys don't know whether to answer with 'present' or 'not guilty.'" Every head in the room nods and smiles a bit. To understand this remark, you've been brought into a ring of familiarity. All of you together share the knowledge of your board, plus the reputation of boards to rub the edge of legality, and for that moment a bond of understanding is created.

Unfortunately, current trends assure us that the path to any selected salvation requires you to get serious and focus. What numbskull put those ideas together? Since when has being grim been a tool to aid concentration? You might better encourage yourself to get clever and focus, so your broadened perspective may catch every peripheral opportunity.

In the middle of a really high-pressure enterprise, do you occasionally find a bit of grave-side humor creeping into your mind? Like playwright Oscar Wilde, who, purportedly on his deathbed turned to his friend and remarked, "This wallpaper is terrible. Either it or I will have to go." If your mind is working that way, congratulations. Maintaining your sense of humor amid a crisis is a good indicator that you probably love what you are doing. And if you are not presently enjoying the swim of your current life direction, please stand strongly and engineer the necessary changes to put yourself on the joyful track.

Touching the Spirit ∾ There are truths you know, that you cannot prove, nor need to. You know that within beats some essence of you – some spirit on which all your marvelous innate abilities, nurtured skills, and principles are fashioned. This is the core that your Self CEO wants to satisfy and unleash.

You understand that this innermost spirit blows the ember of enthusiasm into flame and that until you fulfill this core essence, contentment will forever elude you. The Author of this inner force, and its nature, stands among humankind's most pondered questions. Seeking the divine has

Sustaining Your Corporation

spawned more religions, statuary, song, debate, and printed pages than probably any other topic in our history. But pushing the tomes of opinion aside, in those hours of solitude, you, like most of us, probably feel that it is not satisfying to trek life's journey all alone. You may find strength in the belief that the Author did not just drop in your essence and stride away. It remains. And on comforting occasions, you sense the touch and welcome in that power.

How best to define this force that created and imbues your spirit? That is the subject of your own lifelong debate. Have fun with it. As CEO, you may study and realize the full potential of spirituality and all the beneficial vitality it floods into your soul. Whatever your beliefs, do not deny searching for this asset. It may be shadowy and ill-defined. Like the enriched life itself, the blessings of the spirit remain a process, not a prize. Yet the rewards of cultivating your spirit and connecting with its Author lie beyond estimation.

One of the prime ways to discover your own spirit has proven to come with the act of unleashing it in others. For years, spirituality was held at arms' length by business leaders as an activity that was best boxed into separate holy days. Yet as competition grows fiercely global, the need to inspire the maximum from each staffer has become frantic. Corporate heads, grasping for whatever works, have begun to mine the rich potential of human spirituality. If business is no longer relegating the spiritual quest into one corner of life; why should you? After all, your spirit roams universally through your being; why employ it in only one room of your house?

You have been right from the very beginning. There is a richer experience waiting out there, and you are now seizing some of those tastier parts of life's feast. It is an addictive banquet, and appetite grows with the delicacies it feeds on. The goals you set forth in Chapter 1 doubtless have expanded right along with you. New pinnacles are catching your eye. Obviously, your Self CEO has your work cut out for you. Time to dance. **BB**

Afterthought ❧

Once you paddle a whitewater river in a canoe, you will never look at any flowing water the same way again. In 1949, a group of pioneering whitewater paddlers in the Appalachian Mountain Club lifted their vision. Louise Davis, Corny King, Ruth Walker, Helen Fair, and six others formed an expedition to paddle the Glen Canyon section of the Colorado River, a part of the gorge not yet dammed. Already experts at handling the Northeast's smaller streams, these paddlers prepared for this grand adventure with Yankee ingenuity and New York organization.

An engineer and inventive seamstress, Louise designed canvas boat decks for the aluminum canoes with C-shaped zippers for rapid gear access. Weekly planning meetings were held and organizational charts laid out. Corny King, upon testing the waters, developed a new "pry" stroke and a river-reading strategy he called "following the feathers." The expedition was a thrilling success, which pushed the infant sport forward and changed its members forever. Though you'll never find it in the history books, this adventure is still the stuff of paddling legend. Sometimes, your team is already in place. It only takes your vision and a touch of leadership to galvanize the group into action.

CEO of Yourself

Chapter 13

Beginning Today....

*The best time
to chart a better course is when
glory gilds the skies each morn.*

– BJ

Fate has handed you this day. It is all yours. From the very first episode of my radio show, *The Art of the CEO*, I have posed a reminder and a choice to those tuning in:

As I always do, allow me to remind each of you hearing my voice that the Good Lord has gifted you with the title and privileges of Chief Executive Officer of Yourself. And since that is the most important position you will ever hold in your career, please allow me to ask,

"Will this be the day that you...."

Through each episode, I have continued to put forth one such personal leadership choice for listeners to consider. After all, if you would lead others, you must first learn to lead yourself. So as you are gearing up to further build yourself and take a more fulfilling hold on life, it seems appropriate to send you off with a few final choices to ponder.

Will this be the day that you:

Dust off your dreams and engineer one step toward their fulfillment?

OR

Will you continue to delay your true desires due to more pressing needs?

Take the ear buds out and let your feet, not the channel selector, direct you to the sounds you want to hear?

OR

Will you continue to satisfy your senses with packages preprogrammed by another?

Look back on your week, examine your goals, and see how you'd like to spend this coming week?

OR

Will you continue to take refuge in routine?

Tally up the contributions you've made to those around you?

OR

Get mired in the measures of compensation, wealth, and deserving?

Write down a list of three slightly scary ventures for your long-range planning kit?

OR

Will you continue to keep your eyes riveted to the tasks at hand, with the closest deadlines?

Learn about yourself by asking some special, trusted confidant for an impartial evaluation?

OR

Do you need to find and cultivate a special, trusted confidant first?

Test your absolute limit in some sphere and prove how tough you really can be?

OR

Will you chain yourself to the motto that you cannot be too careful nowadays?

CEO of Yourself

Discover one inefficiency in your daily routine and puzzle out a correction?

OR

Will you continue trying just to speed up the same old process
with the same old tools?

Hold to light one myth that society keeps pushing at you to believe
and then make up your own mind?

OR

Will you meekly accept that 50,000 believers just like you can't be wrong?

Burst the bonds of status and talk to all the people you encounter
as fellows?

OR

*Will you continue to buy into some artificial hierarchy, created
by you or others?*

Dwell for a bit on Your Own Marvelous Self and consider employing
all your many assets?

OR

*Will you continue to throw your precious efforts into bandaging
those flaws that others have pointed out?*

Begin to see finances and possessions as mere tools?

OR

*Will you continue to endow them with some artificial value in and
of themselves?*

Argue for those principles in which you truly believe?

OR

*Will you refuse other people the benefit of your ideas because you fear
disapproval?*

Look to your tools – physical, mental, spiritual – and see which
need sharpening?

OR

Like a dull axe, will you continue to bruise, rather than polish?

Beginning Today....   115

List those individuals who could really help you, then create some benefit to give them by way of introduction?

OR

Will you let lack of creativity, inertia, and shyness keep that door closed?

Laugh at yourself and share the joke with others?

OR

Are you not strong enough to do that yet?

Pick a battle because you know it is worth fighting?

OR

Pick a battle you are sure of winning?

Find the treasure of solitude and let it recreate you?

OR

Push away your personal thoughts with the ceaseless noise of the madding crowd?

Sample all the persuasions of today's media and realize how little you require them?

OR

Will you contort your own vision as each new pitch comes along?

Find something you'd like to build and dive into creating it?

OR

Will you check your to-do list before making a move.

The choice, my friend, is truly yours.

CEO of Yourself

My Thoughts...

A few thought starters, and
a little space to jot down
what's of value to remember.

My forgiveness system for myself includes...

**In my case, the thing that really presses my emotional
buttons and causes an explosive response is...
And the emotion I need to stop repressing is...**

My greatest Broccoli Moment challenging me on my path
toward fulfillment is probably...

The one soul-enriching gift – well, maybe two –
I'd like to give myself is/are...

From this day forward, I can best describe my vision for
the Enterprise of Me as...

CEO of Yourself

The Entrepreneurial Employee

*An entrepreneur launches
his own adventure – it doesn't matter
who signs the paycheck.*
–bj

As discussed in Chapter 9, The Call of Career, the workplace offers expansive opportunities for you – the Self CEO to carve out a path of mastery and creative fulfillment. Yet for a host of reasons, the salaried employee tends to miss more of these opportunities and voluntarily cede more choices to others. Thus, for all those who are swapping their expert services for a paycheck, we offer this pocket guide of examples to make sure you don't forget to carry the Enterprise of You into your jobsite.

She was the new kid in the shop, with no experience, and to make it worse, she was the owner's niece. No one held very high hopes for this upstart. But Shari Spiro seethed with a friendly fire. You could tell by the way her words just came tumbling out as she came up to you and began asking questions, and more questions.

Placed by her uncle at a tiny desk with small administrative duties, Shari took every opportunity to walk the floor, learn each staff member's expertise, and absorb every aspect of the small job printing business. She learned color blending, distribution, sales techniques, pricing, and production methods from letterpress to laser. She wanted to master it all. Shari also devoted countless hours talking with repeat clients, discerning their needs, and giving a face to the service the shop provided.

"In the beginning, it came from a need to prove myself," Shari recalls. "I was determined not to be known as just the boss's niece, given a charity job. But very soon I really got into it...I just found the whole world of printing fascinating, and the business part really excited me." By the end of her first year, staff members began to turn to Shari with their questions. She had become the go-to girl for coworkers seeking an overview or forgotten details.

So what exactly made the young Ms. Spiro stand out? She saw business as a realm of opportunity – not an obligation. Shari had entered into her new situation with an entrepreneurial attitude. By entrepreneur we mean an individual engaged in creating value – someone willing to undertake some exceptional challenges to bring forth worthwhile benefits, including, but not limited to financial gain. Personally, this author always envisions an entrepreneur as any enterprising venturer who is more scared of missing out on the fun of an opportunity, than she is scared of failing at it.

Tucked into Shari's entrepreneurial portfolio were the following assumptions:

▶ I am a talented individual with many things to offer. (I've already toured my mental warehouse and discovered a marvelous, capable self.)
▶ Yes, I also am now part of a team. Each of these folks holds some information that can help me perform better – and perhaps I might discover some ways I may add to their experience.
▶ I want to be – I can be a contributor.
▶ Here is an opportunity for fun and challenge. There's a whole lot of activity buzzing around this hive – interesting people, inventive processes. The more I know about who and what's making it all happen, the happier my workdays will be.

Wisely, a few of the attitudes Shari excluded from her portfolio were:

▶ I'd better be very careful, keep my head down, and make sure I don't screw up.
▶ Focus on my job and don't get distracted by things around me.
▶ I really need this job. The money is very important to everything I have planned in my life.
▶ Every person in this company is my competitor. I need to constantly compare my progress against theirs.

These guaranteed recipes for workplace misery she left safely locked in a closet at home.

CEO of Yourself

Tips & Tasks Shari Spiro's entrepreneurial mindset fed these actions:

▶ Studying the latest printing techniques and discussing them with coworkers. Then, taking their mutually derived ideas/suggestions to the owner.
▶ Examining her assigned projects and determining each's exact role in the entire business process.
▶ Constantly adjusting and expanding her labors to make them more effective with that process.
▶ Developing a mental catalog of individuals' various expertise and resources. ("Jill is the one to help me with this.")
▶ Forging personal relationships throughout the entire workplace regardless of rank. Doing favors – finding after-hours interests.
▶ Giving credit for that exceptional endeavor aimed at improving the firm's product or procedures.
▶ Casually making folks aware of her individual effort and willingness to help.

Do you suppose some of these habits might bring a little zest, benefit, and personal mastery into your workday?

As an after note, when I met Shari Spiro, she was busily plunged into managing the rewards of her entrepreneurial business approach. As will happen in family firms, circumstances shifted. Several years after Shari's joining the company, her uncle, for reasons both personal and financial opted to sell the shop. By mutual consent, Shari took over the business, changing the company's name and direction. Titled Admagic, CEO Shari Spiro and her lean team now stand as one of the largest independent manufacturers and publishers of new playing card and board games. Catering to the more rebellious/fun streak in millennials, the company has brought forth the wildly popular Cards Against Humanity, Exploding Kittens, and other successes too humorous to mention. Her coveted games sell so well worldwide that Shari has developed a 3-D device to prevent international piracy. And Shari still radiates her broad smile and engaged energy that indicate how much joy she is finding in her chosen career.

The Entrepreneurial Employee

The Wage Slave

Of course, instead of launching into your job as an entrepreneur, you can always lapse into default mode, and opt for the Barcalounger approach. Shuffle into your new supervisor's office and greet her with, "What do you want me to do, boss? I'll do anything you ask." While this all-too-popular first-day announcement to your employer may seem ingratiatingly obliging, it is the last thing she wants to hear. In essence, you are reminding her that she has just hired a tool – a mindless worker, awaiting instructions, showing up to serve his time. "Just the thing we need, how nice."

Further, with those thirteen words, you have wrapped up all your chief executive self-mastery and tossed it into the lap of another. All your decisions, your time, your thinking process, and, let's face it, any hopes for pride and joy you have given away. And no, this is not part of your trade, as we discussed earlier. Your trade is the valuable services you perform in exchange for the chosen compensations you require. Your mind and spirit are non-negotiable pearls beyond price.

Blunders to Avoid   And by the way, poverty is no excuse for the wage slave attitude. You may have desperately grabbed your current job to keep a rented roof over your head and put three bowls of rice daily on your children's table. This merely means you are poor, it does not mean you must make poverty your master. All the entrepreneurial opportunities discussed above are equally available to the assistant produce stacker in the local grocery store, as to the CFO of a global tech giant. Your chance to pridefully create value always stands. Got a good idea to share with the boss, or a question for a coworker?

As a young, dirt-poor, African American man, Ken Parker stood in front of Atlantic City Electric's headquarters, walked around to the rear, donned his jumpsuit, and began mowing the grass. 18 years later, Ken again stood in front of these corporate offices. This time he walked in the front door, greeted all his coworkers, chatted with his administrative assistant, pushed open the door marked "President" and dropped himself down in the huge leather chair behind his desk. Another day of keeping more than half a million families in the greater Philadelphia area electrically empowered.

Ken's mind-boggling rise rings with the aura of a romantic, Horatio-Alger fantasy. He was the first in his family ever to graduate, or even attend, college, and certainly the first to obtain such a leadership position. But once you meet the man, it becomes obvious that there's a lot more at play here than some allegory of sweat and naked ambition. Ken Parker took a markedly different entrepreneurial approach to his career. He exhibited an almost terrifying laser concentration on each task set before him. "You could always tell when Ken has cut the grass," was the common remark around Atlantic City Electric. It was a sense of powerful pride that fed his ownership of each undertaking throughout his vocation. Lawn maintenance was not an assignment. This was Ken's personal responsibility which, by heaven, would reflect the kind of person he was.

Secondly, employee Parker held a vision. He took to heart the mission of his company and, like Shari Spiro, actively built a solid understanding of all the workplace processes around him. "Each time they gave me a new assignment," Ken recalls, "I would make a list of all the departments and individuals this job would effect. Then I'd go around and ask each one how I might differently perform my job to make things work a little better for them on their end."

Tips & Tasks If you wisely want to undertake the Parker-performance-networking system in your own workplace, why not actively take notes as you listen to the needs of your coworkers? Let each one see you recording her ideas. And, oh yes, don't forget fulfillment, and followup.

Your Three Promotable Products

Business is a juggling act. Whether you are on an existing firm's payroll, or you are desperately trying to generate revenue from a venture you are launching, you are still an entrepreneur – out there creatively creating value. And this means you have three separate, yet connected value sources that you always hold in your mind to promote and push forward.

1. Your Marvelous Self   You are performing your own work, employing your own tactics. You are that individual who is always thinking, concerned about his coworkers, coming up with good ideas, and bringing beneficial things to the firm. The responsibility falls on your shoulders to connect your many deeds with their author. People need to see the value you are generating, so that they will give you the respect you are richly earning every day. (Hint: Self-promotion is a subtle art. Your deeds alone may not speak for you. Some brief reminders and quick mentions on the fly always seem to work better than leaning in with diatribes on the greatness of your grand efforts.)

2. Your Company   You are part of a team. You have committed yourself to these other men and women, and their corporate goals. Just as you individually stand for your personal principles, the company you have joined has its mission, and its unique culture. What elements of these make you proud to be working here? Yes, of course, there are some bozos and bullies, but which leader and coworkers are performing so admirably that you can boast about the connection?

3. Your Product/Service   You have made yourself aware of all the benefits of what the company brings forth – as well as your part in the creation of these benefits. You have talked to the clients and discovered how they profit from what your company offers. 'Tis only natural that you want to share those benefits, for the sake of your own pride and the good of the community. If you truly search and find nothing good about what you're selling, you have two choices. Either labor to make that product worthwhile, or get the heck out of this company before you spiral into a self-loathing cynicism.

None of these three items stands in conflict with one another. Pride, like love, is not a fixed-amount emotion. That pride you hold in the company you've chosen to offer your services, will feed your personal value and raise the esteem in which you hold yourself. Likewise, the enrichment your product brings to the clients and the community at large is also a personal value enhancer. After all, you personally are contributing to it. It's success is yours. Just remember, sales are not the sole measure of value. Even if the buyers haven't caught on yet, your brand's safety, quality, durability, or whatever your niche, all reflects favorably on you.

Tips & Tasks   Like it or not, you (and every other employee) will become the spokesperson for the company at which you work. Those people surrounding you will grow to know your company through your eyes, and your reports. Now, I don't know a darn thing about tractors, but after five minutes listening to John Deere worker Wanda Sano, I wanted to buy a John Deere. I even wanted to work for her company. No, Wanda wasn't in sales; at the time she was guiding executives through the labyrinth of her firm's computer technologies. She simply believed in her vocation and the product towards which she contributed. I still don't know anything about tractors, but I'll bet 10 cents of my own money that Ms. Sano, with her vision of the value she's adding, heads her off to her job with an energy, fun, and pride that most of us would en$. Have you found any source of pride in your workplace and its team?

In the Corporate Swim

As we have noted, being an entrepreneur is a mindset, not an activity. Your mindset of innate curiosity and inventiveness can lever you out of workplace loathing, up into workplace enthusiasm. That said, it all becomes a lot more complex when you step into a massive corporate entity.

Financier Warren Buffet noted that it is difficult to judge your accomplishment within a large corporation: you always wonder if the company is like a train bustling along at sixty miles an hour while you are sitting still. You try to keep awareness of your individual contribution to the firm's progress and products, but it may appear remote and hard to trace. You try to be inventive, but however brilliant, your innovations can get lost in protocol. In business, all too often, big means sluggish.

The good news is that the entrepreneurial mindset scales easily from little shops like Shari's to multi-thousand-employee corporations, like Ken Parker's Atlantic City Electric, Inc. Regardless of company size, you take full engagement in the three value entities of your work: self, company, and products. The opportunities are still there – more often greater. But the engagement process requires some extra steps and research.

First, catch the company rhythm. Just like joining any new business, you begin building a solid understanding of the processes – who does what in your area, how do things move, through whom. Buzzworders today call it the culture. But the firm's rhythm is more dynamic – less tangible. Does this company operate with a steady, legato, thoughtful flow – or do things surge in staccato jumps? And if these moves come suddenly, what and/or who is conducting this rhythm? Do board meetings make the company ship come alive on a new course – or is it the economy, or seasonal sales shifts? In short, you are not just scrutinizing how things get done, but determining why. Discerning this rhythm will indicate the leadership's goals, along with the optimum time and method for making your ideas heard. If possible, ask to audit a board meeting. Even if your supervisor refuses the request, he'll take note of your interest.

Secondly, cast your study beyond your company, and catch the industry tempo. Most high tech businesses (though not all) stride hell bent on disruptive innovation. New decisions are best – rapid decisions are even better. Insurance providers, backed by centuries of process and success, generally move with greater reluctance. The easiest way to seize a strong sense of industry tempo is to attend a few professional organization gatherings. Count on it. As you stand there listening, the tune of your industry will be sung loud and strong.

So what does this have to do with my entrepreneurial self-mastery? Well, as Chief Executive Officer, it is your job to fully assess your circumstance. You may hold powerful assets, and you may be aware of them. But where you deploy that personal capability depends on the currents of the stream you've stepped into. If the majority of your industry is banging the innovation-today drum, yet your company moves with traditional caution, what is your best strategy for promoting yourself, your firm, and its products?

Entrepreneurial Checklist

When it comes to exploring and learning about the company you have selected to receive your many services, the process remains fairly similar, large or small. Invest your time and meet every individual you can. Learn who does what. What's their problem – what's their expertise? When are their birthdays? How many kids are they feeding? What do they know that you need to? What could you do to make their job easier? What's their favorite lunch/after-hours place that you're going to invite them to learn more? Oh, and don't forget that you are feeding more than your business self. Look for new friends, folks engaged in common interests, and yes, even romance. (The world is a tragedy for those who only think.)

However, in the larger corporate setting, you and your firm occupy a greater portion of the economic stage. The more you know about your industry as a whole and its place in the national/global commerce picture, the more valuable you become and the more people in decision-making positions will want to talk with you.

Knowledge held in a state of readiness, at any level, transforms you from an assigned-job worker to an asset. A few of the tongue-tip answers you will want to keep abreast of include:

▶ What is your company's stated mission?

▶ What is the firm's revenue? What is the current trend? What prime streams are most responsible for this income?

▶ What are the prime products that are bringing in the revenue? Who is buying them and what is their selling niche (e.g. is your product the cheapest, highest quality, best known, most convenient to local customers, etc.?)

▶ How do these brand values and sales figures compare with the competition? What's indicated by these figures?

▶ Looking at recent industry trends, who is succeeding and why?

▶ Fun Facts – Your firm has a triple retention rate of similar firms in the industry. More leadership roles are filled by humanities majors in your company than researchers or engineers. It never hurts to pose a few fascinating stats to liven up discussions and lighten the mood.

Finally, last mentioned, but vitally at the top of every businessperson's exploratory checklist comes **The Customer**. The most effective entrepreneurial strategy I have heard in all my years came from Arizona State University Professor Scott Livengood: If you have it in mind to start an enterprise, go sit down, face-to-face with 20 people who might use/buy/benefit from your product, and listen to their needs and ideas concerning what you have to offer. Not three, not five, not 20 interviews seven years ago. This is more than customercentric showmanship. You are going to be devoting your brain and sweat into this enterprise. You need to keep constantly calling and learning from those folks who did buy that product you've helped make – as well as those who didn't buy. Yes, we mean making personal phone calls to strange, valued clients.

Taking Pride

Your pride is a sin only to someone who sees it as a threat to their own individual gain. As CEO of your marvelous self, pride is one of the greatest sources of personal reward and encouragement you will discover on the job – or anywhere in life. As the entrepreneurial employee, this means clutching at pride in your personal accomplishments – those of your company – and those of its products. Your ideas and achievements remain truly yours. Company owners supplying you workspace and salary may compensate you, but they cannot own you, nor should you let them hamper the contagious pride they create in you.

Donovan Klotzbeacher, working for the Agricultural Department's inspection division, spent his days at the New York port checking the incoming cargo for invasive pests. An irrepressible tech wizard, Don invented a program which weened all the inspectors away from using paper manifests, onto a faster, sharable, computerized system. The Secretary of Agriculture personally thanked Don, and a small bonus was involved, but that was all the official recognition.

If you lay pipes along a roadway, end to end, you had better be sure those ends are precisely cut so that each length lines up perfectly flush, or you may be sending water off into the next county. Warehouse worker Marvin Arroyo spotted this hazard, as well as the flaws of the existing systems. So he invented a wooden mold that assured a perfect cut for each length of pipe going out of his workplace. Marvin's boss thanked him profusely, set him on the top of the overtime opportunity list. And Marvin went back to work.

Unlike Shari Spiro or Ken Parker, the world did not open for these two entrepreneurial individuals. Neither ended up growing rich or taking board of directors' seats. Instead, each won the admiration of the most important person in his life – himself. And if you would like to see justified pride at work, glance over at Marvin or Don when they stroll through the office/warehouse and see their inventions in use. Theirs is the compensation of the entrepreneurial employee. 'Tis an opportunity potentially available to each person entering the realm of business. Yes, Self CEO, we mean you. ▣

It is my sincerest wish that you have found something within these pages that has helped you take a greater pleasure in yourself and in your life. As noted in the Introduction, the pathway to that enriched, fulfilling feast of days is strewn with broccoli as well as baklava. The work is often hard, and the guarantees few. Ah, but the rewards of your quest are intoxicating, and hopefully they will inspire you onto your next summit. Doubtless you have realized that this is a book of choices. As is your life. May yours always bear the fruit you seek.

And because every long journey grows easier with companionship and a friendly guide to lean on, I would personally like to offer you any possible further assistance in your quest. If you would like to chat or seek counsel at any time, please feel free to drop me a line, and we may arrange a connection. BB

Wishing you every success,

Bart Jackson

CEO of Yourself
Info@BartsBooks.com